the real meaning of life

the real meaning of life

edited by David Seaman

New World Library
Novato, California

New World Library
14 Pamaron Way
Novato, CA 94949

Cover design by Mary Ann Casler
Interior design by Tona Pearce Myers

Library of Congress Cataloging-in-Publication Data
The real meaning of life / edited by David Seaman.
    p. cm.
ISBN-13: 978-1-57731-514-8 (pbk. : alk. paper)
1. Life. I. Seaman, David, 1986–
BD431.R33 2005
128—dc22   2005012899

First printing, September 2005
ISBN-10: 1-57731-514-6
ISBN-13: 978-1-57731-514-8

Printed in Canada on 100% postconsumer waste recycled paper

A proud member of the Green Press Initiative

Distributed to the trade by Publishers Group West

10 9 8 7 6 5 4 3 2 1

For all those who have ever stayed up late at night, tossing and turning, asking the question we all must face.

You will never be happy if you continue to search for what happiness consists of. You will never live if you are looking for the meaning of life.

— Albert Camus

Introduction

I'm afraid you might have picked up the wrong book. You won't find a glossy cover with some well-dressed guy towering triumphantly over the embossed promise of his book. You won't find a day-by-day checklist for improving your life. You won't lose any weight. This isn't Prozac in an easily digestible paperback format. Please, don't waste your money if all you want is another self-help guide.

This book is about the meaning of life. What could be more important? The meaning isn't always pretty, but it is almost always enlightening.

Let me step back in time for a moment. It is the fall semester at New York University. I am a freshman. I have just failed my second calculus quiz in a row. I have a ton of acquaintances, but few real friends. My Barnes and Noble discount card is dangerously close to expiring. In sum, my life is not steaming ahead at full speed. Oh, and I'm at a Starbucks, where I am supposed to be writing a long paper on God only knows what. (No exaggeration: the paper was about God and the cosmic order in Dante's universe.) Instead, I am doing what any responsible student would be doing: surfing the Internet on my laptop. In a moment of despair, I type, "What is the meaning of life?" into one of my favorite online forums and hit Enter. I expect the usual level of Internet discourse: a handful of nonsensical responses written in broken, abbreviated English.

To my surprise, when I refresh the forum page fifteen minutes later, there are forty responses awaiting my attention. Within an hour the number grew to sixty — almost all of them deeply insightful commentaries on the human condition. Sure, a few people suggested "bikinis and beer," but they were in the definite minority. This particular online forum only stays on a theme for a week. Then the discussion is deleted or moved to some archive I have never been able to locate. I desperately wanted to receive more insight from everyday Internet folks. So I created a bare-bones website at www.realmeaningoflife.com. This is what it said:

At some point in your life, you're going to look for meaning. Maybe at eighteen, maybe not until you're seventy-two.

Let's face it, you have no idea what's going on. Neither do I. I am soliciting advice on the meaning of life. If you have a few words of wisdom, email them to meaning@ shutterline.com. It can be a few sentences, a few paragraphs, or a few pages. Include your full name — or a nickname if you prefer anonymity — which I will publish along with your response. Just don't send a link to the Bible. Or to that Baz Luhrmann song about wearing sunscreen. Be original but useful to your fellow human being. Suggestions for making the world a better place are also welcome. Thanks!

To make a long story slightly less long, people really liked the sincerity behind my request. They started to submit answers — advice for making life more meaningful — and encouraged their friends to do the same. It was only a matter of time before publications like *USA Today* found out about the site and wrote about it. This significantly increased the number of submissions.

What follows are some of the best entries received during the seventy-six days the project was open to submissions. (Of course, I did end up including some passages from the Bible.) I have tried pretty hard to keep my own ideology (whatever that may be) out of the way. Most of the responses are uplifting and positive, if only because life is intrinsically a good thing. I have included some more pessimistic entries as well. Who am I to argue that we are more than just intelligent cell colonies? I can hardly get a C in my calculus class! One visitor wrote, "Life is a sexually transmitted disease that is always 100 percent fatal." Way to ruin the party for me.

The entries are in no particular order, so you can read from beginning to end. Or from end to beginning. You can even randomly turn to a new page each day for inspiration and provocative family discussion. It's sort of like those commercials for Reese's candy: there is no one right way to eat them. The same applies to the consumption of *The Real Meaning of Life*. It's totally up to you, what with free will and all. This is not a textbook ruled by logic and pie charts. Many, if not all, of the entries included draw on the life lessons of individuals. With each approach to the question, we get closer to the answer. The truth is in the sum of all the entries combined. May this book benefit you as much as it has me!

David Seaman
New York City
Spring 2005

What Is the Real Meaning of Life?

When I started attending the University of Tennessee at Knoxville, my parents made me do a work-study program. I got stuck in Sophie's cafeteria. An incredibly irritating guy there developed a crush on me. One day he really needed the evening off and begged me to take his shift, even though I only worked mornings because it was an hour's commute from my parents' house. Against my better judgment, I took his shift. That night, as I was helping to close, the manager sent in a guy to help me put chairs on the table so I could mop the floor.

Eight years later, this coming Thursday, in fact, we're still married, with two kids. All because I took an extra shift at my shitty job.

— **Barbara Kilpatrick**

friday morning, waking up in the arms of someone you love, it's raining...so you call in sick to work (giving yourself a three-day weekend), go back to sleep, and at noon ordering chinese, eating lunch in bed, and watching cheesy reruns all day while the world drags on without you.   — avk

The meaning of life is...
Life.
Here's the longer version:
All life exists to re-create itself. Blast an island to dust with a volcano, and within a few years stuff is growing all over the place. Why? Because it *must*. Follow the chain up from RNA and you get replicating organisms. Why are we here? To reproduce. We eat so we're strong enough to have sex. All else is justification.

— **Doug Finner**

Life is short, and the end is always unknown...and closer than we think. What on earth can you *do* with this time? What would make our time on earth worth the trouble?

Some people go to religion. We are predictive animals; we see into the future. And when we see our death, we can't accept that we will no longer exist. So religion fills that void — life after death, reward for all our rights, and punishment for all our wrongs.

Me? I just don't see it. The big guy in the sky seems far too implausible.

How do I go on? How do I continue to respect and honor my friends, live a good life, and try to improve myself? Why? What is the point, when it will all be soon forgotten?

I don't know.

What I do is I learn. I learn how to make things. Creation by my hands. Computer software, jewelry, robots, balloon animals, the written word, humor, compassion. I create everything I can, as often as I can, without interruption.

A better answer would be that to live is to love, and to love is to bring more light into the world. If we are to suffer this brief interlude, we might as well do all that we can to make the burden light for ourselves and for those around us.

And who knows? Maybe there is more to it than what we can see with our body's eyes. We can only hope.   — **Edwin**

I've been to the top of the pile, sank to the deepest depths, and seen every point in between. What keeps me hanging on? Morbid curiosity about what will come next. Life is an experience, and there's always something more, good or bad. The trick is learning to take both with equal reverence....   — **E. James Jacobson**

Having just survived my fourth heart attack, eleven months of unemployment, and a divorce not of my own making, all within the last year, I think that life means the following:

Love those who mean the most. Every life you touch will touch you back. Treasure every sunrise, every raindrop that hits your nose, every slobber of your dog, the feeling of sand between your toes. Be moved by the tears of a child, and try to fix the cause. Be grease, not glue. Breathe deep, exhale slowly, and never miss a chance to help another while on your journey here.   **— Don Stephens**

Beer, ribs, professional sports, and Miles Davis.   **— Mike Barber**

Waking up early one morning in a hotel room. Walking down the hall, through some doors, down more steps. Then realizing that you can run away right now and never be found again. Feeling truly free.

Wandering around London. Always having a general idea of where you are, but at the same time being kind of lost. Lost in a sea of people you don't know.   **— Adam E. Heller**

Humans generally seem to be goal-oriented creatures. I really hate it when people write cover letters for their résumés saying they are "goal oriented." It's completely pointless to say that, because everyone is goal oriented. It's just that some people have very different goals. I have a friend whose goal is to get married before she leaves her childbearing years. I have another whose goal is to be filthy stinking rich, and yet another friend whose only goal is to make it to the next day. I think the third friend is the most realistic and perhaps the sanest, though perhaps a little lazy. It's true that in life there are be-ers and doers, but the be-ers have it right, in my humble opinion, because spending all your life running to get to the same place everyone's going anyway too often causes you to miss out on all the really nice things the world has to offer. All the hard work you do might bring you great wealth, which will allow you to buy all kinds of *stuff*, but does that "stuff" really add to your life? One might guess the guy sitting in a $3,000 massage chair watching a 50-inch plasma-screen TV has a better life than a sugarcane farmer who sleeps in a shack where the only entertainment is the sound of crickets chirping at night. But how many of these so-called comfortable people are actually happy? I would guess that those farmers are often experiencing life on a level the man in the massage chair can only dream about.   **— E. J. Sepp**

Roughly 10 percent of life is spent trying to shirk death. The rest of life is probably spent waiting in line at the supermarket.

— Tishon Woolcock

If you see a big ring of fire ahead of you and it scares you half to death, jump through it! It is only our fears that veil our true identity. Conquer these and you'll find what's left of you is love, a love so brilliant that ten thousand suns would not be your equal. We are all searching for truth, we all want happiness. Learn to love yourself and these gifts will follow. Stop looking outward...the answers lie within. And for God's sake, stop grazing in the fields of chaos and fear that the media is cultivating for you. Fear sells, and we're buyin'. You are more powerful than you know. Enjoy.

— Jack Dempsey Boyd

At the end of the day, it's not that complicated. We're here on this planet for a short time. Appreciate every moment. We have a sacred responsibility to appreciate the opportunity of this life and make the most of it. There is an integrity to pursuing your dreams that animates all other aspects of life. Aim to leave the world a little bit better than you found it, whether it is through something as small as standing up for kindness or as big as building a movement to bring about broad change — both take courage. Be the change you want to see in the world. This is harder than it sounds. It is still worth pursuing.

A lot in life urges us to give in to the arrogance of the moment — the assumption that opportunities will be here forever, so why bother to take action? Do not listen to this domestic devil. The opportunity is here and now. To paraphrase Goethe, boldness contains the seeds of genius — take the first step today. Words and intentions are important, but ultimately actions matter more. Some people are lulled into false comfort or confusion by diffusing their sense of responsibility. One way to shake off this complacency is to look at a present challenge through the eyes of history. Imagine how an issue will be seen in twenty years, and the right decision will usually be revealed. Generational responsibility is the bottom line. After all, the deeper purpose in politics is that you get to participate in making history in the present tense.

Remember that worry is a waste of time and that fear is not your friend. There is a temptation among some good people to overthink to the point of paralysis. This does no one any good. It is true that the unexamined life is not worth living, but it is equally true that the overexamined life is also not worth living. Instead, as someone once said, "Think like a man of action, act like a man of thought."

Enjoy challenges: identify and embrace the responsibilities of your time. After the attacks of September 11, I worked for a time at the New York City Office of Emergency Management (OEM). Anxieties were running high about the possibility of another terrorist attack. This often translated into indulgence in a nervous parlor game in which all sorts of horrific attacks were imagined. On a metal bookshelf in OEM's makeshift offices under the Brooklyn Bridge (the original offices had been destroyed with the World

Trade Center) was a line of binders detailing suggested responses for the City to a full range of doomsday scenarios. And yet, while people in taxis contemplated fleeing the city or upped their dose of Paxil, the cops and firefighters who worked at the OEM went about their jobs and daily life with a sense of purposeful calm. They had a saying: Hope for the best but prepare for the worst. The trick was not to worry — that was a counterproductive luxury they could not afford. Instead, keep focused and hold on to your sense of humor. Be fully prepared, and look forward. If something comes up, then deal with it.

At the end of the day, we're all in this together. As Jackie Robinson once said, "One life is not important except for the impact it has on other lives."

As I write this, I'm in an airplane looking out the window at the endless clear-blue horizon above thick clouds, and I'm reminded of the importance of perspective, how nature reminds us that there is always a blue sky above the clouds. Likewise, leaves fall off trees at the turn of the season, and plants appear to die after the first frost, but come spring they bloom again. Pain always comes before a child is born. The sunrise and sunsets in life are sublime, and every night we see that it is darkest just before the dawn, but on a deeper level we know that the sun never actually goes down — it's just an illusion caused by the world spinning around. Nature is nudging us, offering fresh evidence for hope and faith, love, and persistence against all appearances. It still takes some courage to step confidently into the unknown, to seize the day and shape our future, but we should appreciate the process and enjoy the ride.   **— John P. Avlon**

Life is a cocktail. It consists of various measures of family, relationships, play, and work. Our quest, should we be prepared to accept it, is to find our unique mix. Every decision we make alters this mix. Learning from our choices and making corrections as necessary will enable each of us to find our perfect cocktail.

— "Sir Percival Blakeney"

Let's start with you. What does *your* life mean? That you are alive means that your parents loved each other enough to make you. That you are alive means that your parents loved *you* enough to let you live, in spite of how annoying you were. That you are alive means that God thinks you will do some good, either for yourself or for others, that would go undone if you were to die this instant.

What does God consider good for you? The answer is, everything that happens to you, if you let it be good for you and teach you something. If it weren't good for you and God didn't think you could handle it, God wouldn't let it happen. Even things you struggle with can be good if you overcome them, because they make you stronger. That's how you can do good for yourself. It would be tragic if you were to let yourself be overcome by things God knows you are capable of handling with his help.

What does God consider good for you to do for others? A major part of the meaning of life also has to do with what you make of it and how you perceive it. Further, you demonstrate to God what the meaning of your life is by how you live it. What you spend your time on conveys what you *really* think means something, religious convictions notwithstanding. If you spend your time on things you feel are meaningless, life will seem meaningless to you, and you will probably be pretty miserable and discontented. If you spend your time on things you feel are meaningful, then your life will be full of meaning, and you will be pretty happy, no matter what happens to you.

Life is meaningful when it is worth living. Life is worth living when you help people. There are many different ways of helping people, and life is most worth living when you help people in some special way that only you can. A very quick and easy example is this book. No one else has come up with the idea of asking people this question in quite this same way. You are helping people by asking a *very* important question and asking for answers from everyone. Because you expect everyone to respond, people do, and forming a response requires that they think seriously. Whether they send you a serious response or not, the thought they put into the subject may start them on a search for more meaning, so it has the potential to benefit many people. I have no doubt you will help lots of others in your future, so the meaning of your life is not going to end with this project.

Another aspect of life with an enormous amount of meaning is the struggle to acquire as many good character traits as possible and to rid oneself of as many bad ones as possible. It is a lifelong struggle, and it is very rewarding, but I am afraid too many people deny that such a struggle is worth it with the excuse "that's just the way I am."

All I can say is it feels so good to have rid myself of one frailty that I immediately start on getting rid of the next one I discover in myself. To sum up, I think that the meaning of life lies in three things:

1) love

2) service

3) building good character and destroying bad character

God bless!   — **Michaela Stephens**

What we call coincidences have happened in my life. I don't know how or why, but they make me think that there is intelligence or order to life. In the same way that the small lumps travel to the bottom of a packet of cereal if you shake it, like seems to attract like.

That feeling I had about which estate agent had the house I then fell in love with, even though they didn't normally advertise that type of house? Like attracts like.

Life can be beautiful, and life can be cruel. It can be difficult when you see abhorrent images and hear disturbing stories. And the whole point is that there isn't an answer to this. It is a moral and ethical paradox, in the sense that we can never resolve it to our emotional satisfaction.

Conflict exists.

But it is possible to realize that life is a paradox and to live from that perspective. You can't deny your feelings, positive and negative, in the same way that you can't deny the positive and negative things in life.

Living is as much a responsibility as it is a gift.

I spent my twenties looking at religions and philosophies. I think of myself as a Taoist, but I'm a lot of other things too. Because I have a pragmatic outlook on life I find my joy in life through work. I enjoy my work, and it suits my mind. Not everyone is the same.

I read something recently that said that it is healthy to have changing values. It quoted a mathematician's cat that preferred fish

to chicken, chicken to beef, and beef to fish. Tomorrow I might
believe something else.   — **Anonymous**

This is what I have learned. I hope it makes sense, even if you don't
agree with me. All that I ask is that from this moment on you listen
to the love of God and the growing love of the soul within you.
You don't have to give up material things and join a monastery. You
only need to learn to love as best you can. I don't mean just to love
people. Love sunsets, bass fishing, pool, orange juice, cats, Gauguin
paintings, everything else. Just love and love and love some more.
Love with all the passion you can muster. By all means help yourself to the gifts that this life affords you. Enjoy them to their fullest.
You are meant to have them, whatever they are. Whenever practi-
cal, help yourself in other lives. Accept who you are in this one.
That's all.   — **Ralph A. Gessner**

I've been thinking about the meaning of life as it relates to our
impulses.

The problem with understanding oneself is that being a part
of oneself prohibits accurate observation. To use an example,
an object must be pushed by an outside force for it to move. Have
you ever stood on a skateboard and tried to move yourself with two

feet on the board? Through accurate counterweighting you can achieve a minimal amount of movement but hardly enough to get anywhere.

The mind is such a complicated beast that it prevents itself from understanding itself. Dreams are a gateway to understanding, as your subconscious acts as another voice. Drugs are another way to think outside the box. It is fascinating, though, that drugs are only a crude shortcut to something we are all capable of. Through discipline we can control all the automatic functions in our body. We can even make our hearts stop, given enough force of will and training.

I find it amazing how my mind and body work. The levels of neurotransmitters and nutrients in my system determines how I feel each day. Sometimes I try to control the way I'm feeling or try to focus my mind and find that I just cannot. Or sometimes I find that because I just ate a really healthy dinner I'm at a peak of creativity.

I've always thought that it doesn't take a smart man to find the meaning of life. Sometimes all it takes is happiness. If you are truly happy in life, then you are closer than I at finding the true meaning.

Serotonin is a chemical in your brain and body that determines your level of happiness. It makes you feel at ease with the world and helps you to understand those around you and yourself. When you fall in love, your serotonin levels shoot up. It is amazing that drugs that affect serotonin, such as MDMA, 5-htp, or any of the SSRIs like Prozac, can make you feel better about yourself. It's funny that the same chemical that controls your happiness also controls your body heat, your hunger, and your exhaustion level. The happier you are, it seems the more energy you have.

Life isn't just as simple as serotonin levels, though. All the serotonin in the world won't make you feel fulfilled forever. Countless other factors are involved, but I'll give one more, dopamine. This is the chemical in the brain that makes you feel good after you accomplish something. The rush you get after winning a tough competition, getting a raise, or otherwise achieving a tough goal comes from dopamine. Most addictive drugs affect your dopamine levels. All cocaine does, for example, is affect your dopamine levels. You feel like you did a good thing after you did the cocaine, which causes the addiction. This is also why cokeheads tend to be full of themselves. These neurotransmitters are responsible for many other things in your mind and body than their main purpose.

I think it is obvious that we aren't meant to be happy all the time. If we were, we would end up, oddly enough, unsatisfied, and ultimately we would die from lack of sleep, food, and so on.

Being bipolar, I've come to an understanding that we must be happy, and we must also be sad. It is a duality of life, to borrow from Taoism. You must have sadness to have happiness. Without sadness there would be nothing to measure happiness against. There would be no accomplishment or feeling of greater connection to other human beings.

Since the chemicals in my brain are all out of whack, and I go from one extreme to another, I think I experience the dual nature of life more than some. The more manic or happy I get, the more depressed I get later. But usually the depression isn't a bad thing. At least I don't think of it that way anymore. It is a kind of downtime when I think about the other factors in life and truly appreciate the wonderfulness of life. It is also a time when I prepare for my next bout of mania.

Life is full of unexpected ups and downs. At times we all get caught up in the rigors of it. It is important to take a step back sometimes and see the humor in all our emotions and reactions to things. If we can just take that step back, then we can find the meaning in each situation and come closer to understanding the meaning of life.

Understanding the meaning of life comes from experiencing all that life has to offer. If you truly feel, truly love, truly hate, truly live, then you can begin to understand the purposes of your brain and the nature of things around you. Attempting to merely think out the meaning of life will get you nowhere. Your mind is not about to give away its secrets.   — **Dave Brown**

I'm a twenty-year-old, so my view on life is still somewhat...hazy. I need to live more. I don't know if I'm being original — if I'm not, at least I arrived at this on my own — but I think that the real meaning of life is "to look for the meaning of life." It's not a circular definition — I'm just saying that the generalization of something this profound is wrong.

Six billion people in the world, all different from the inside out, *might* have something in common, but the meaning of life? It should be more like "what's the meaning of *your* life?" What are you? Why are you here? What are you looking for?

I'm still looking for my purpose, and I believe that's the meaning of life: to look for it.

— David Yim

Maybe if life ran in reverse, it would be better. You start old, reeking of piss, in a dingy old people's home, ignored by your loved ones. Then life gets better as it goes on. This still isn't much better than the beginning, but at least you'll be wiser on the way through!

— Mark Kennard

For me, the meaning of life is to leave the world a better place than you found it. Many of us will come and go, leaving ripples that fade over time into the noise of history. A select few, though, will play the role of chaos theory's butterfly. Through actions that perhaps even appear insignificant, they'll kick off waves of change that leave a lasting impression on the landscape of human culture. I hope that somehow I manage to start some waves that improve the human condition over the long term.   **— Hans Gerwitz**

In the continuum that is eternity, life is consciousness merely blinking.

— Jim Paredes

Life has no meaning, but as humans we try to associate a meaning or purpose so we can justify our existence. People try to look to their future for a meaning, for a direction in life, when they should be looking to the past. If you look back on your life and smile, you have had a meaningful life. If not, you haven't. Simple.

— Mathew Thompson

In 1991 I went shopping with a friend at an antique jewelry and clothing store in southeastern Virginia. While she shopped for jewelry, I browsed around the men's clothing section, with an eye on suits to purchase. I was going to college at the time and living at home, and I knew that the summer job waiting for me required more professional dress than jeans and T-shirts.

The black, pinstripe suit that caught my eye was only $42. The tag read "1960s," but it was a classic suit that wasn't out of style. I tried the jacket on — it fit perfectly — and the pants, which needed to be hemmed up a bit. I bought the suit and took it home and hung it in my closet.

Later that day my mother asked about the suit I had purchased, so I tried on the jacket for her. She told me that it looked good and felt the lining of the jacket to judge the quality. She reached into the inside pocket and pulled out a small white card. She read it, and I read it, and we honestly did not know what to make of it.

It was a National Honor Society membership card from Portsmouth, Ohio.

I stared at the card with a bewilderment I can still vividly recall, many years later. My mother doesn't believe that the card was in the suit when I bought it, but I do. I do because I went back the next day to the shop where I bought the suit, and I asked the owner about it. She told me that she got some of the clothes she sold from her sister, who owned a similar store in Wheelersburg, Ohio.

Wheelersburg, Ohio, is just a few miles away from Portsmouth, Ohio, where I was born.

The name typed on the card was Bill Atkinson. My father, Bill Atkinson, died a few months before I was born in a boating accident on the Ohio River. After he died, my grandmother gave some of my father's clothes away.

It was my father's suit. Five hundred miles away and twenty-two years after his death, I had bought my father's suit.

Now, if you can't find some meaning in that, then I don't know what to tell you.   — Ted Atkinson

We are memes, genelike, self-propagating units of cultural evolution that act like Trojan horses, smuggling bits of psyche into our consciousness. The result? We become more conscious of the unconscious material "at work" within us and around us.

— Michael Glock

I believe in God, just not in some kind of organized-religion way. I think he created us as an experiment. I think we provide a great deal of entertainment for him, too. I have no issue with this, because his motivations for creating us don't prevent me from doing what I would do anyway. I'm grateful, really, because if he hadn't come up with the idea to create us, I wouldn't be here. I wouldn't have experienced the joy of tasting chocolate, or beer, or sometimes both at the same time! I wouldn't get to sit around and wonder about the meaning of life. But I get to do all of that and more, and I think that's really cool. I just think we owe it to him to do our best not to destroy ourselves. Since I think we have to do this on an individual level, I try my hardest to do the right thing, without being sanctimonious about it. I have a somewhat twisted sense of humor sometimes, but I don't think God cares about that, so long as I'm mostly nice.

As a believer, as much as one can be, in reincarnation, I believe that heaven and hell exist on earth. My current life is the afterlife of my past life. I can choose to make this afterlife heaven on earth. Since I understand that this is how it works, I'm happier than most people.
— **Heather Kennedy**

To me the meaning of life has to do with your reaction to life. It is all about being there for a friend in need or even just having a smile on your face for all to see. It is about not getting weighed down by life's trials, but rejoicing in the victories, no matter how big or small. Did you get to the gas station before you ran out of gas? Victory! Were you able to make someone smile today? Victory! Did you find out that your cancer is now in remission? Victory!

— **Kristy L. Hodson**

Life is simply a paradox. A paradox is a problem that cannot be solved with rational answers. For a paradox to exist, it must be in "thought," meaning that someone must be trying to solve it in order for it to exist.

This is much like life . . . it only exists if you live it.

To get a better understanding of things, one of my high school teachers always told me to look at the situation from a different perspective, angle, view, and so forth. Over time, we have all gradually learned to accept our view of life as the only view possible. This means that life is how you perceive it. We have no other "takes" on life, so it is difficult to say exactly why we are here. Basically, all we know is life itself — nothing more.

So, the meaning of life?

Well first, what *is* life? Humans call their existence life. Basically, life = existence.

So the question can be: Why do we exist? This can be "answered" by explaining the contradiction of existence, which makes life a paradox.

Think of space. Technically, the universe is a vacuum. A vacuum is nothing. So, we exist in nothing.

We exist in nothing…that is the simple paradox of life. Life is nothing, but everything. So, you ask again: What is the meaning of life? Here is my answer. Life is the meaning of life.   — **Artur Borys**

In a word: love. Not the Hallmark kind of love, but the deep, abiding stuff that holds us together, the bonds of fellow-feeling that keep our hearts from cynicism and bitterness. Love of family, love of friends, love of long summer evenings and bright winter days, love of music, love of strawberries, love of that creaking sound the rocking chair makes, love of beaches, love of football, love of all the earth and each person on it. Love of life itself.

— **Matthew Penniman**

The meaning of life is to forget about the search for the meaning of life.   — **Christopher J. Peterson**

It cannot be put into words. It is something you feel at certain moments: when you are fully present with a loved one, or with a tree that enchants you, or completely at one with yourself. It's an experience, not a concept, and it cannot be held onto in time.

— **Joel Rosenfeld**

At the age of forty-two (Douglas Adams's answer to the Ultimate Question, no less), running a bookshop, studying for a master's, married (my second go, and at ten years, longer than the first), Christian (in that English way of yes-I-am-but-let's-not-get-silly-about-this), the father of a eighteen-year-old, and the step-grand-father of a three-year-old, I find that my philosophy of life is this: always be open to the possibilities. Anything's possible in both the best and worst ways you or I can imagine, and well beyond that. I was in Seattle on September 11, 2001, to speak at my oldest friend's wedding the following Saturday. They went ahead with the wedding — his family couldn't travel, but everyone else got there — and we all felt it was important for this to say something about life and being alive. Anything's possible, and you have to be ready and willing to deal with that. Always keep an open mind, and an open heart. Yes, make decisions, even the tough ones, but do so with the knowledge that nothing lasts forever, nothing stays the same, and that what actually happens might just turn out to be better that your original plan. Live life to the fullest — carpe diem, as older, wiser heads once said — and take advantage of every opportunity that comes your way. Oh, and never knowingly turn down free food.

— David Simpkin

To me the meaning of life is for us, as individuals, to find our own equilibrium: find what makes us happy, what balances us, what keeps us healthy, what makes us vulnerable, what gives us power, what drives us forward, what holds us back, what motivates us, and what brings us down. Sometimes it is an activity, a thought, an image, another person, a country, a philosophy, a religion, a cult, a book, a film, or a website. That's what is so great about the question: it helps us question our own individuality, our relationships, and our own definition of ourselves.

— Kate Losowsky

The meaning of life is to throw a small object into the sea and create a tsunami.
— **Danny Wolfman**

Life is short in relation to time. Yet a specific amount of time is granted to us. It's been said that from the minute you are born you begin to die. That, of course, is but one way of looking at it. Then again, why is life created if it is only meant to end? Why is it that our bodies last only so long and that resources are limited? Why is there disease, plague, famine, war, murder, suffering, and the question *why*? Who instituted laws of nature, like gravity? Why do the planets circle in the manner they do? Why do the seasons come and go without wavering? Why are we placed in the city, the country, and the circumstances that we are placed in? Better yet, why do we feel remorse over and sympathy for the tragedies mentioned above? Why is humankind attached at the heart? Why is it that you can fall in love, marry, have a family, and be connected to another individual mind, body, and soul? What are friends? Who are your friends? Why do we have enemies? Why have I envied and hated? We have so many questions, and it seems not so many answers.

By the meaning of life, do we mean the *sense* of life? Or perhaps the *significance*? What about the *purpose* of life? That one is easy. The purpose of life *is* purpose. Life is created for purpose. One purpose, or many. Do we all find our purpose? We can.

How else can we explain the control around us? But that it is for certain purpose, of he who is creator. Why do certain events in time happen when they do? Because it is a "will" being performed.

Find your purpose; it's not hard. It's written down for you. It is written in your heart and in your soul. It's what binds you in affection to others. It's what makes you feel awe at the inexplicable wonders of nature. It's what calms our hearts and elevates our minds. My purpose is to serve. I'm a messenger. I'm a servant. Peace.

— **Aaron Patino**

I have to confess that I'm addicted to the WB's *Jack and Bobby*, and after only two episodes. I can already see it quickly following the likes of *My So-Called Life* and *Freaks and Geeks* into a one-season cancellation, despite cult uprising — it's too intelligent to survive. The show follows two teenage brothers growing up in contemporary America — one of whom grows up to become a visionary U.S. president. The construction of the show is ingenious, charting how one's upbringing subtly shapes the values of his future character. The tagline for the series is what hooked me from the beginning: "Would you recognize greatness if it was standing right next to you?"

It's common for us to want to believe in destiny. The first half of Bill Clinton's memoirs is a terrific read because it appeals to this sense. Examples of this include when Clinton's first-grade teacher told his mother that her son would grow up to become president or the infamous encounter of young Clinton and JFK in the Rose Garden.

Over the summer, I read Michael Bamberger's *Wonderland*, which chronicles the lives of several high school seniors at a Philadelphia high school and pinpoints exactly what it is that makes high school seem like such a distinctive time in retrospect: "Is there a time when fantasy is richer? You're old enough to see a real glimpse of your adult self, but young enough to dream. Somehow you meld the two, the glimpse and the dream."

I remember how many conversations with friends in my class revolved around what we would make of our lives. Chris Moore would be a basketball star. Brandon Huseman's band would go platinum. Fallon Carroll would be the first woman elected president. Now it's only two years later, and already it seems to me that we're all letting ourselves compromise. We used to want to take over the world *and* be happy — now we just want to be happy. Are we more realistic or just lazy?

I was a pretty big overachiever in high school when I didn't have much competition, and I knew that the Rotary Club was just waiting to recognize me for it. Now that I'm adrift in a sea of more than twenty-eight thousand people who don't care if I nap all day, it's getting increasingly difficult to do anything. My apathy crept in so subtly I never noticed it.

Compare the idealism of the fictional candidate in *Jack and Bobby*, or even arguably Clinton, with the 2004 presidential candidates — two men who once were lowly undergrads themselves. They went to more pedigreed institutions and had more affluent upbringings but for the most part were no different from the strangers sitting next to us in astronomy class. And one day, someone who is currently sleeping through astronomy at Pitt, Yale, or anywhere is going to announce his or her candidacy for president of the United States.

In kindergarten, we were told that we could grow up to become whatever we wanted. It's still true. Let's make sure we stay in touch with our friends and that we walk away from college with plenty of good memories. But let's not allow the weight of our dreams, whatever they may be, to crush us.

Our whole lives we have been angry about all the things we were too young to do: too young to ride the big roller coaster, too young to watch *Die Hard*, too young to drive, too young to drink. Our time is finally here. We can go off to Iraq. We can cast our ballots in November. And we can begin to build the future. In a few years, however, we will wake up to find that we are in charge. I want to make sure that I feel good about where I have ended up.

I don't think national politics is in the cards for me, but I do intend to hold on to my dreams for as long as I can.   — **Daron Christopher**

Take a seat on your neon starship waiting to take you away, and gaze up at it in wonderment. Float on a river made of chocolate roses and daffodils, only to find that childhood memories are only a dream. You sit in an absentminded trance without knowledge of your location. The world is flat. No, that's not right, but who is to say? Live in a theoretical lie set up by society's long-past ancestors. They will rule you. Learn from your mistakes, but don't learn too hard. They will kill you. Think of all the things you can do in life, but don't think too hard. It will destroy you. Pull in a treasure, but not one too big. Save your riches in your heart, and keep your materials in your head for another day, when all is lost. Hop on your concrete balloon and set sail on a closed plain. We are all free.

— **Jack Gassensmith**

Living each moment to its fullest. Never expecting to see the next instant. Counting on nothing. When you say good-bye to someone, leave nothing unsaid, nothing unheard, and nothing undone. Have no regrets. Do nothing you will regret later. Regret nothing. Do not live with the expectation of growing old, or older, because you could die the minute you walk out the door. Life is acknowledging that death is inevitable and unavoidable.

The universe. Picture this. A proton is made up of quarks; so is an electron. Many of these make up an atom. Many atoms make up a molecule. Many molecules make up a cell. Many cells make up an organ. Organs make up an organism. Organisms, and other things made from the same path, make up planets. Planets make up a solar system. Solar systems make up galaxies. Galaxies make up stellar clusters. These make a universe. Maybe there is more than one. Whatever the case, it is all contained within a single quark. All things are connected, all things are relative. Things work in circles.

Everything. Everything has a place, a purpose. Maybe your purpose isn't what you think it is, or would like it to be. Rest assured that whatever your purpose is, you will fulfill it just by existing. Maybe you're meant to take over the world, maybe you're meant to cure cancer. Or maybe you die alone and cold in your house, thinking you've never fulfilled your purpose. But then, as you close your eyes, you remember that last week you gave your favorite baseball glove to a poor kid. That kid grew up to be a famous pitcher. Everything has its purpose, and every purpose is just as important as every other purpose.

People. People are different. Science has proven this. No two sets of fingerprints are the same. No two strands of DNA have the same coding. Don't expect someone, even your kids, to be just like you, because they won't be. The only you is you. Don't try to force anyone to think what you think, or believe what you believe. Opinions and beliefs are just speculations; nothing is 100 percent proven. Love everyone, and everything, equally and unconditionally. Even if you don't agree, respect other people's beliefs and opinions. They will do the same, in the end.

I may be wrong. I probably am. But you know, there are worse ways to look at things.   **— Sephiroth Evangelion**

There is no meaning to life. At least, not in the way we romanticize it. Does anyone ask what the meaning of life to a deer is? A fish? A dog? A flower? No. It is pretentious for human beings to think that we are so far removed from and superior to other life-forms that our existence has some special "meaning."

I believe that the true meaning of life for humans is the same as it is for any other species; eat, excrete, play, and procreate. Humans spend way too much effort and time contemplating the meaning of life. If you want to make life better, stop wasting your time analyzing something that shouldn't even be a question and *live* it.

Live life so that you can do what makes you happy, whatever that may be.   **— Aleesha**

People love and hate each other, and nothing changes that. We argue right or wrong, your fault, my fault, you owe me, I didn't mean it, this is what your problem is, but all we're left with in the end are pure emotions. Millions of years of evolution, and it's still that simple. We try to harness our emotions, reserve certain feelings for certain people, but it doesn't always work. Communication is so complicated, but in the end, we're communicating the same things we always have.

Compatibility, and working things out, will not always subdue our instincts. When we work things out with each other, we're agreeing on ways to feel what we want to feel without hurting each other. But we can't just eliminate our crazy feelings. Keep that in mind, and I think many things in life will go much smoother.

— Benjamin Paul Schuman

What's funny is that sometimes you find that the most clichéd sayings are actually the truest. What's the meaning of life? To live life to the fullest? To be all you can be? To make an impact on as many people as possible? To change lives? The fact of the matter is, the answer is all of the above. The meaning of life is whatever you want it to be. The meaning of life is defined by each person, each mind, each soul. Because we cannot know for a fact (by our standards for what we define as true) why we exist, everyone will define for themselves what life means to them. Therefore, *the meaning of life is your meaning of life.*   **— Brian J. Hong**

So often I am troubled by this notion of the "meaning of life." I steadfastly believe that to presume the existence of some broad, all-encompassing meaning behind the life of humanity, so often sought in religions or spiritual relations, would be to neglect the necessary realization of ultimate personal autonomy that is more careful and rightfully reverent of an ultimate self-dictating meaning. In other words, the meaning of life is not God, nor is it accurately life itself. Nor is it "the good," or happiness. Instead, the meaning of life is defined by the self, in answer to the call of what one is to do with it.

Consider the statesperson. One person's passion for politics may indeed not be for the backslapping adventure found in most competition but instead in the self-expression of a quasi-altruistic sentiment and drive for the realization of some greatness in the conscience of people within a nation. Therefore, it can be said that while the point of one person's life may be sport — factual, social, political or personal pursuits — it might not by necessity apply to other such people. By way of true irony, it seems that many of those who struggle between the predigested nuggets of others' work in considering the question of life's worth and meaning are so often the very ones who, by virtue of maintaining a state of life-lessness, will never find the meaning of it.   — **Matthew R. McNabb**

The meaning of life is finding happiness and love and making a dif-ference. It means to fight to be your own person while the rest of the world tries to pressure you into being one in a crowd. The meaning of life is finding meaning for yourself.   — **Tina Guo**

Life. Ha. We are living to die. We wake up from this little ball of mucus, pop out of someone's privates, and start crying our eyes out. Probably the best cry of our life. There's a lot of emotion there. Then a lot of firsts start happening. First piece of real food. First time you ride a bike. First time you fall in love with that cute girl in third grade. First kiss, even if it is at an amusement park. First time you have sex. First time getting drunk. First time getting high. First time you get dumped by the girl who "loves" you. First time you dump someone who loves you. First time you get a job. First paycheck. First time you get fired. First million (well, not for all of us). First marriage. First kid, and now your progeny goes through the exact same stuff you did. Then there are things that can only happen once, like each year, each birthday, retirement.

But what is life but a bunch of firsts? Things can only happen once. You can eat the same meal every day of your life, but it was still yesterday's meal, and well, tomorrow is tomorrow's meal. You can only fall in love with someone once. You can continue it, perhaps it is an "eternal flame," but you can only meet them once. You can only go through high school once. And you can only go through college once, technically. So my advice is this: when you are going to do it, do it big. Do it to the edge. And when you are taking it slow, take it real slow. Because there are no second tries.

— **Andrew Forbes Winkler**

Humankind has been around for over a hundred thousand years. If we haven't figured out the meaning of life by now, we're either asking the wrong questions or we're too stupid to realize the answers. Either way, sometimes thinking is as fun as it is futile.

— **Laura Kyle**

Isn't it fascinating that we always ask questions like this?

"What is the meaning of life?"

"Why am I here?"

"How can I be happy?"

The questions in themselves are never any comfort, because we, in all our curiosity, can never be happy with only questions and in this way are separated from all other animals.

The deer does not ask why the river flows or the hunter strikes. The bugs do not ask why the pollen must be spread for life to exist. Only human beings could ask a question such as, "How can I exist?" or, "What is life?" Perhaps the only answer is in the question itself.

Yet what is life but the processing of a sensory input by the brain to produce a reality? And if our minds are capable enough to create a reality without any input at all, as it is in our dreams, then how can we know we are not dreaming now? How do we know that we shall not awake somewhere else, in another time, in another life entirely?

The important thing is not the answer, because life is not about answers but about the fact that we can even ask the question.

A man once asked me, in Spanish, the only question worth asking: "¿Porqué?" (Why?)

I answered him with a smile, knowing that in asking, he may never find his answer.

"Porque." (Because.)

The question is the answer is the question. And if you're confused, then you may have finally begun to awaken.

— **Joshua Levinson**

I don't know about the meaning of the life for others, but I know about my own. I am only eighteen, but I feel that even though I don't know where my life is headed, I know how I want to live it. I am not religious; in fact, I am a definite atheist. I feel that knowing there is no afterlife makes this life even more precious. The meaning of my life is to bring joy, truth, and affection to the lives of others. To demonstrate my dedication, originality, and appreciation in all that I do. To approach life with curiosity, responsibility, and enthusiasm.   — YellowJ

How does one define life? Fun, boring, easy, hard, pain in the ass, waste of time? Life is what we make of it; it is as simple as that. We have nobody but ourselves to blame if we are unsatisfied with how we are living. True, there are elements we perceive as working against us or keeping us from reaching the stars, but in the end it is up to us to make the best of what we do have control over. If you can make the most of the time you are given each day and go to bed each night with no regrets and keep a smile on your face through the hours, then you are indeed alive and that, *that*, is life.

— Justin Cohn

I returned a year ago from a trip to Israel, only to find out that a friend of mine had passed away in a major car crash. He did nothing wrong; he was simply in the wrong place at the wrong time. I thought back and realized that only two days after his death, there was a suicide bombing in Tel Aviv, where I had been two days prior. That could have been me. Yet I was having the time of my life. So I thought, "What did I do wrong that I should live and he should die?" Nothing.

What have I done since? Moved on. I'll never forget him, but I have my own life to live, and if I don't, then I have no right to be here. If it was me who had died that day, I know of at least a hundred people I would have never met, another country I would never have visited, and countless friends who would mourn my death. I lived and am living. That is the meaning of life.

— **Jared Paul Baker**

I had a high school teacher who would say that all we want in this crazy world is to love and to be loved. I always wanted to deny it and think that life's meaning was so much more, but the more I think about, the more I can't argue. As cynical and as bitter as we can be, all we really want is to love and to be loved, whether we know it or not.   — **Cassie Harris**

Telos, the idea of some ultimate end, is perhaps the most misleading concept ever crafted by human minds. For humans are egotists, always attempting to stamp their own consciousness onto the universe at large. They cannot understand that their ultimate telos is to be human — that is, is-ness is all that it requires. Giraffes are yellow and black; humans are conscious. However, we mistake the information that consciousness gives us as ontological truth rather than a subjective reaction to the universe. Our searching for telos is accounted for in the flow of the universe, but our telos can never encompass the totality of the universe. Rather, in our simple being, in our simple truths, we reflect and emulate the way. The ultimate truth is to be, to cease reflecting on it and live it. Our reflection is accounted for in the way — one can never go against it. We deviate from it when we do not realize that we *are* it.   **— Christopher Taylor**

Nothingness is the answer. Once you realize this fact, your life will be complete. You will be. You will no longer be troubled by anything. Some have called it nirvana. Others have called it heaven. It is both these things and also neither. It is a moment in time. A fragment of the awesome consciousness that is life. Everything has a meaning. Think of this tomorrow as you enter into a new life. Dichotomies are useful. Fear nothing. Embrace everything. For nothing is everything and, in an ideal world, everything is nothing. That is the struggle that consumes our lives, from the greatest rich man to the feeblest pauper. Enlightenment is achievable, if one only follows the path of nothingness.

Harvard professor Tal Ben-Shachar claims that happiness is the ultimate currency. He is right in this estimation, but only halfway. Happiness is half of the ultimate currency. The other half is misery. The ultimate is only achievable through the unity of these opposites. That is the answer. Synthesis! Zero sum. Uniting happiness and misery, or any two seemingly illogical ideas, will cancel the two out and create nothingness. The pinnacle of existence. No tension. No doubt. Just being.

Others have arrived at this conclusion before. However, they have misidentified the necessary steps to reach this ultimate conclusion. Moderation has been preached before. Yet one cannot achieve nothingness through moderation, for truly not only does the journey determine the destination, but it is the destination itself. To achieve nothingness, or pure being, one must first embrace the extremes necessary to achieve nothingness. To deny such extremes would be to deny the very meaning of existence. Thus, we see the answer that is before us all the time. Nothingness is the meaning of life. Embrace it.

            — Samuel Sanker

Your first step is to understand that life is suffering.

A shitload of suffering.

Now comes the fun part!

Do the things that make you happy. Eat that whole cheesecake. Get ridiculously drunk on a weeknight.

Forget what others think of you. At the end of the day, do they wash this body of yours? All your nooks and all your crannies? Do they have any idea about the burdens of life that you wake to? How could they possibly *begin* to understand what goes on under your folds of skin? You *are* the one and only, the best.

Love the people you love, practice witchcraft, buy the things you want, have that illegitimate baby, as long as you'll love him or her with everything you've got. Renounce God if you don't have faith (apologize to your parents, thank them for trying to save your soul, but explain to them that you are searching for the meaning of life, and this is the only way). Pursue art or music as a living, even though you know that's not where the money is. Live on top of a tree in the rain forest so that it doesn't get cut down.

Do whatever you want. The world is your plaything.

Before you die, leave most of your estate to your favorite people and descendants (if you have any). But if you have extra, you should donate a significant sum to a charity with a cause that you truly believe in (think hard; there must be at least one).

And finally, now that you are dead, you must suffer the consequences of enjoying your life.

Suffer away.   — **Melissa S. T. Eng**

We do not know any better than to try to fulfill our desires. The struggles to satisfy all these desires are impossible because of contradictions. This struggle is known as life. Our feelings and emotions manipulate us into submission, a set of directions that we follow without knowing it. The end product: evolution. The ability to restrain pleasures at will puts evolution in our hands.

— **Matthew Brent Lipman**

"Feeling."

Sincerity evident in their eyes, others say, "I hope you find whatever it is you're looking for." I say, "I hope so too." I hope so too, because I haven't yet found that sense of spiritual balance. Equilibrium I cannot reach, for I continually teeter as I walk the line between the known and the unknown, understood and misunderstood. The desired universal truths and the unwanted weight of that knowledge. Too often others grow warm and comfortable in their seats of unquestioning. I cannot. I continue tightrope walking over the lands of dissent and compliance, curiosity and resignation. Please never allow me to submit to the cooling breezes of a "settled" life. For I never wish to merely settle. Let me bleed and let me ache, just do not ever let me go numb. True, sometimes I wish I could stop feeling, but in the end I know the pain will always be more welcome than the unfeeling. Feel. Question. Never concede to mental or spiritual stagnation. For the meaning of life lies in the investigation itself, not in the answers granted. **— Rachel Rudwall**

The most important thing to remember is that life is not set. Many times people think of the meaning of life as a specific goal we are supposed to achieve. That is as faulty as considering death the meaning of life, for if death is the only definite in life, then it should be our only goal, since everything else is transient to us as corporeal beings. Life is simply what we as human beings make of it, so it becomes a sort of study in human nature to find what we want and do with life.

Remember, it's the meaning of life, not the meaning of death.

— David Zwerdling

"*Insignificance!*" the saddened, defeated souls cry. We mean nothing, they say. We are nameless faces swimming in a pool of indifference, infinitesimal flecks spotting the incomprehensible portrait of the cosmos. It does not matter, they claim, if we die now, or in five years, or in fifty years, because our existence on this planet dies when our bodies expire. That is, if we cannot remember our lives when we are dead, why live at all? Should we stay alive for others, to "make the world a better place," to impress some monumental change on the human race? Should we live only to affect more lives that are equally insignificant? They scream these hopeless words with passion, and if they could actually *feel* that passion, perhaps they wouldn't speak that way at all.

Our understanding of the world, indeed the nature of how we recognize ourselves as beings at all, is dependent solely on our inner experiences, feelings, and perceptions. We never escape our minds. The world is only as real to me as I perceive it to be, only as real to me as I wish to make it. If my experiences are all I have, then they are the only things that should be of importance to me. It should not matter that the world will go on without me, because I will never experience the world when I am not living in it.

In truth, life itself is all we have, and because of this, it only makes sense to fill each moment with beauty. *This* should take precedence in our everyday proceedings. To do nothing, to believe that life means nothing is the true failure, the most scornful declaration of ingratitude for the wonderful blessing of conscious freedom that we have been afforded. Meaning in life is determined by how we choose to experience the world, not by how the world experiences us. *It does not matter* that we will die and perhaps remember nothing of this world, *it does not matter* whether we are remembered or not. It only matters that we enjoy our experiences. We must realize that we are all born with the freedom to put whatever meaning we'd like into our lives.

The impact I have on the world is not something I can experience, but it *is* something that I can allow to trouble my experiences. So many people forget about the importance of their own happiness. To live is what is important. It is all I have. It is all you have. The meaning of my life is determined completely by me. You can be utterly happy if you allow yourself to be. You can make your life meaningful, if you want to. — **Amanda Schmidt**

The meaning of life is different for everyone, but invariably it appears when one isn't looking for it. We gain no perspective by constantly looking inward; we also become disoriented and unhappy. Only when we dedicate ourselves to an external pursuit, something that engages our mind and our passions, will we discover what gives our lives meaning. — **Amanda Johnson**

It can't be getting anything man-made, like money, cars, or houses. These things have only been around for a tiny part of human existence and most soon won't be.

It can't be just to assuage the basic drives, life food, sex, security. They're the only goals of primitive animals and even lower life forms.

Leaving what?

What only humans can do and get a kick out of doing: thinking and imagining — and, in the far future, maybe more.

— **Ray Dickenson**

There is no prescribed meaning of life, since human life is one of the few intrinsic goods. It is good on its own, not because it is a condition for achieving other good things.

The meaning of life is simply to live. People must create their own meanings based on their experiences, values, and beliefs. Then they must pursue their meanings with absolute passion. To do anything else would be to deny the importance of their own existences.

While there are some flaws in their thought, the existentialists were on the right path when they said that existence comes before essence and that we are what we choose. Until we learn to make rational choices based on our experiences, we are nothing but a lump of biological matter, no better or worse than a puddle of bacteria. It is these choices that make us human and allow us to give our lives meaning.   — **Paul R. Welke**

Some define it by the amount of worldly possessions they can acquire in this lifetime. Still others believe that it be can be found in the walls of ornate churches and synagogues. To the poor, it is as simple as providing shelter and food for themselves and their families.

Hindus believe that a spiritual energy exists within every person. This energy is described as a dormant serpent sleeping at the base of the spine, waiting for the day when it will be awakened or released. This is known as "kundalini energy." When this energy is released, you are thought to be enlightened. When you are enlightened, you possess the knowledge of the ancients, which helps you to understand your existence.

The ancient Egyptians believed that preserving the body guaranteed a prosperous afterlife. They also preserved the organs of the body by placing them in special containers called Canopic jars. Interestingly enough, the brain was thought to be a useless organ and was destroyed. They believed the seat of all knowledge was within the heart.

Many people only believe in their physical existence. They believe that, as the scientists say, if it cannot be measured or weighed, then it does not exist. You must believe in the spiritual energy that exists within you. If you do not think that it is a part of what makes you an individual, then how can you find it?

In the Gnostic Gospels, found in Egypt in 1945, are ancient writings believed to have been composed shortly after the death of Christ. Who wrote them is much in debate. Many think they are the direct teachings of Jesus. Hidden within the verses are messages or hints on how to obtain enlightenment within your lifetime.

One such scripture is the Gospel of Thomas, in which Jesus

supposedly said: "If you bring forth what is within you, what you bring forth will save you. If you do not bring forth what is within you, what you do not bring forth will destroy you."

This knowledge is locked away inside each of us. To open this spiritual awakening, you must look to yourself. You must be able to quiet your mind of all thoughts to view yourself without a self-protective wall, commonly known as the ego. Unfortunately, it is not as easy as it sounds to have no thoughts while conscious and awake.

Sometimes this release of energy or knowledge occurs by accident; other times people have meditated all their lives in hope of achieving this goal.

Many different religions explain what they believe is the key to finding the answer to why we exist. The description of this energy may vary, but the means by which to obtain this spiritual energy are all the same.

Another quote from the Gospel of Thomas says it well. Jesus said, "Let him who seeks continue seeking until he finds. When he finds, he will be troubled. When he becomes troubled, he will be astonished, and he will rule over all things."

We live in a time of spiritual awakening around the world. Many more people have chosen a spiritual path in order to find the meaning of their life. For the few who have found it, the searching has ended. For those who have not, "seek and you shall find."

— **Amelia Maude**

It seems that my idea about the meaning of life has changed every year since I was fourteen. (I'm currently twenty-eight.) It has jumped from born-again Christian believing I was here to "fulfill God's Plan" — about as vague as one can get — to thinking there was no God and it was all about personal satisfaction, to believing in reincarnation and that I have many lessons to learn, each one bringing me closer to being like the Dalai Lama — about as happy as a person can be.

At twenty-two, my dad was so high on acid he thought he was Jesus. He thought that everyone else was a figment of his imagination and he was the only one left on earth. He cried out to God, "If you are there, you better come save this man because he is going down." And God did. My dad is now a pastor working on his second doctorate in early Christian history and has written a book entitled *Gatebreakers*, a manual on how to witness to those in other religions besides Christianity and convert them.

When I was twenty-two, I was completely disillusioned and called out to God, "If you exist, please show me a sign." The next day on the way to work when I stopped for gas, the attendant was adamant that I look at that morning's newspaper. On the front page was a picture of his brother's fish, which had the marking of Allah on it. At work that same day, a man walked up to me and asked if I believed in God. At a bar the next night, an ex-boyfriend came up to me to tell me that the reason he had mysteriously broken up with me was that I was unsure if I believed in God.

I believe in God now. But my experience was very different from my father's. I believe that the point of this life is for each of us to find the kind of life that truly makes us happy and to pursue it. We each have a responsibility for our own life and our own actions. "Life, liberty, and the pursuit of happiness" is not the same as life, liberty, and happiness. You are free to try to make yourself happy, but no one but you is responsible for accomplishing that goal.

So, wake up every morning, breathe in deeply, pay your bills, meditate, paint, ride bikes, drive race cars. Whatever it is that brings you joy, *do it!* No one else will do it for you. There is no afterlife, so you better enjoy your dessert now.   **— Amber R. Fleming**

Most people think there isn't a difference between the "meaning of life" and "my life's purpose." I am convinced that they are one and the same, but some people are driven by the wrong purpose. Everyone has chosen something to worship. On the negative side, we worship alcohol, drugs, fame, money, and sex. On the positive side, we worship love, good deeds, and improving ourselves, the positive purpose of most world religions. On the *truly* positive side, we worship the One who makes us perfect — and slowly we become better people — less stressed, more calm; less fearful, more peaceful; less angry, more loving; less selfish, more selfless.

My purpose is to worship God. I know I was created to do it, and I am so thankful I know it. Even though it looks like I think God is the meaning of life, in my heart I believe that *love* is the meaning of life, and hallelujah! God is love.   **— Rose Duryee**

Communication — because that is where we have advanced over our animal counterparts more than anywhere else. So the more we increase our means and methods and modes of communication, the more we grow as a species. That is why the Internet and freedom of information and art and ideas are so important; it is also why censorship should be so violently feared.   **— Jason Maronde**

I am only eighteen, and I never really took the time before to think about this question. There was always something happening, and it didn't seem like the right time to reflect. But I have been taking some philosophy classes in college, and it helps to put things in perspective. I am a little conflicted about what I think and how that actually comes to be in the real world. First, I will tell you what I think.

I have all these grandiose notions of what I want my life to be. Certain levels that I have to reach in different aspects of my life before I can consider it complete. Or at least, I used to have these notions. I mean, these things were far-away goals, like making a certain amount of money or reaching a certain position in my company or getting married and having kids. But they were also things as diverse as wanting to live without a home for at least one year and wanting to be remembered. Of all that stuff, the one that sticks out in my mind now is wanting to be remembered.

Every one of us wants to be remembered. We all desire, at least sometimes, to be immortal. This is something that has been in the minds of people for as long as there has been history. It fueled Ponce de Leon's quest for the fountain of youth, and it is the ultimate reason for and backbone of our belief in the afterlife, whether it be literal, in the Greco-Roman sense, or religious, in the Judeo-Christian sense. It is the reason that people have portraits of themselves commissioned, the reason that people want their names on buildings. We live with that eventual goal in mind: to ensure that we, or at least some part of us, live forever.

This feeling pervades every facet of our existence. I am not being so presumptuous as to say that this quest for immortality is the primary motive for all our actions; I am simply acknowledging that we take it into consideration all the time. Whether this consideration is an active reflection or a subconscious notation, there is no doubt that it exists. It is one of the reasons we want children: to ensure that part of us lives on. It is one of the reasons that people make works of art (pictures, sculptures, books, music) or want works of art made about them.

But what it comes down to is that everything does not have to happen on such a grand scale for your life to mean something. You do not have to have accomplishments on par with those of Thomas Jefferson or have enough artistic talent to rival Michelangelo. We were required to read a book at my college before coming into freshman year. We read Annie Proulx's *Accordion Crimes*, a novel about groups of immigrants to America, and we were supposed to discuss the book with other members of our freshman class. The mediator of my group asked us if we thought the immigrants had successful lives. One kid said they did not. He claimed that their lives could not be considered a success because nothing anyone in the book ever did amounted to anything; none of their goals was ever realized. Every one of them died poor, unhappy, and lonely. And a lot of people in my class agreed. But I thought then, and I still think now, that this was totally wrong. Those things matter, but they are not essential to life. Just the fact that someone has learned something from their mistakes, or if someone — anyone — mourns their passing, or if they had a child, or if a loved one changed because of them, or even if the land they lived on has been altered in some permanent manner, that means that they have had an effect on the world during their lifetime, and there is nothing more really required of success. The fact that you made another person happy, that you brightened someone's day, that will never be forgotten in some dark, secluded area of someone's subconscious mind. That will be your legacy.

Once we accept this as the end result of all our lives, we understand why history is so important. It is not the amalgamation of dates and times, persons and places that have passed. It is the record of all our lives, every failure and accomplishment. Figuratively, it is the dipping of our existence into the River Styx. It makes permanent our immortality. It makes life meaningful.

— **Neel Bhuta**

Sad is the day for me when I realize I am alone. As I lie here on the bed, I am not detached. On the contrary, I realize my attachment. I am sad for so many reasons. Sad to be leaving my love, sad to be leaving my childhood behind in only a matter of days, sad that so many things have not worked out the way I planned, sad that I am not the perfect image of myself that I would like to be, sad that I am not perfect in the eyes of others, sad that my ideas are not accepted, sad that I have not found my equal even in the man that I love, sad to be away from my mother, my source of unconditional love and devotion, sad that it was so difficult for me to visit my father and that I didn't realize until I was leaving what he means to me.

Overall, I feel overwhelmed by the intensity of my feelings for others. It is not solely the idea that at all times I am away from someone I love, but also the difficulty I have showing these people how I feel, and that I fear losing them every day. It is strange to me that intellectually I can understand and even explain my theories about death and acceptance, while emotionally, and in everyday life, I cannot apply these concepts. I believe that if I could just accept that everything in my life will go away — those I love, my looks, my possessions — I could find happiness in the simple enjoyment of these things while they are here and not need to mourn their inevitable loss. I think that maybe I'm indulging myself by dwelling in sadness.

I realized the other day that while I may have people whom I would consider very important to me, those people may not feel exactly the same way about me. If only I could show them how good my intentions are, show them how much I care, maybe they would love me back. Maybe not.

I used to think that there were some things about me that would never change, things I would never learn, never be able to encounter. I came to this conclusion solely because I couldn't fathom how I could come to these realizations, how I could be taught, how I could learn, but I now realize that the essence of life is in what you can't predict — not only what happens by chance, but the things that happen because of your choices.

— **Ashley Casselman**

Look up at the night sky and tell me how you feel. What about the Manhattan skyline? Makes you feel insignificant, huh? That's the thing — you are.

Your vote doesn't count, nor does your effort to recycle every last aluminum can. Your personal morality will have no effect on the world as a whole. In a sea of people, you are but one in billions.

But that shouldn't dictate the way you live. Human beings have instincts and emotions — love, lust, anger, happiness — for a reason. Live the life you are supposed to live and follow your heart. In the end, none of it matters; but by recognizing your insignificance and disregarding it at the same time, you will be an enlightened and enriched human being.   **— Michael Devlin**

The meaning of life is riding the subway at 3:00 in the morning, only to see a crack addict pissing all over the thick, yellow line and having the wherewithal to look the other way. As your glance shifts, you glimpse a herd of rats, migrating across the tracks, and, holding back a squeal, you sit on a bench, only to find that you've just stepped in a puddle of vomit.

These repulsive moments can overpower even the strongest of minds. The meaning of them is quite frequently lost on all of us, as we wade through the gore, stress, and monotony clotting our everyday lives, hoping that eventually we will be able to kick off our rubber rain boots and make it to the promised land, where life will somehow be better. Where we can escape a world in which the wealthy investment banker breezes past the starving street urchin, sitting on the filthy pavement scratching their flea-bitten dogs. Where we can lean forward on the democratic spectrum, and connect the underground tunnels to the looming penthouses, breeching the gap between the haves and the have-nots.

As I meander through this wounded city, I strive to find explanation for the plague of poverty miring our streets. Is it karmic retribution for the sins of past lives? Am I living in a hell for the damned, whose eternal punishment is to be forever strung out, face buried in the pavement, watching the Via Spiga shoes of the upper class stomp on their cardboard signs begging for help? Or is this my own hell, where time constraints and deadlines and other tests prevent me from helping them in their struggle through the labyrinth of a decaying island?

Walking home from the gym a few weeks ago, I encountered a $10 bill, folded into quarters, staring up at me like a beacon on the sidewalk. I am not a big believer in spiritual callings. In my opinion, if the clichéd verse "everything happens for a reason" were true, then what would the ultimate purpose of free will be? If our lives are mapped out in a classic Hollywood cause-effect narrative, with God stepping into the Hitchcock silhouette and issuing a deep-throated laugh as he plots each of our existences, then what kind of choice do we have? I refuse to be a marionette. Yet still, as I knelt down to pick up the money, I saw a path springing out from Hamilton's face, and I saw that the small fortune was not merely destined to buy my dinner that night.

I kept the money in my right-hand pocket for the next three weeks, not knowing what to do with it, but under the assumption that I would eventually become enlightened. The moment came as I was sitting in the park, eating a bagel. I casually glanced over at a man in a dust-stained sweatshirt and jeans sleeping on a bench. As I approached him, kicking my way through a flock of pigeons feasting on a piece of white bread, he stirred from his slumber, and I was momentarily taken aback.

"Sir? ... Sir?" I said, but he merely nodded back into sleep, and I knelt down beside him. I wondered what had brought him to this bench — what he had done the night before, the day before, the year before? But we were on two different planes of reality, leaving me in no position to ask. Instead, I slipped the bill, warmed from my palm, into his right-hand pocket and walked away briskly, asking no more questions. I wondered what his reaction would be upon awakening, and what he would spend the money on. My youthful idealism tempered the realistic idea that it would go directly to drugs, alcohol, or some other substance to numb him from an excruciatingly cold night, but I knew this was probably the case. Nevertheless, this escape hatch, the numbness he would experience, would come from me. That was the meaning of the money, that was the meaning of my life for those three weeks of pacing around wondering who would inherit it, that would be the meaning of his life upon awaking to spend it. For a brief blip in this world, a connection was made, and that meaning sustained us for only ten seconds. Who knows where the meaning will come from tomorrow.

— **Rachel Basse**

What if there is no meaning to life? What if, in the words of some fifteen-year-old wearing foundation three shades too light and lipstick four shades too dark, there's no purpose for any of us? That's a pretty dismal thought, my young goth friend — one I don't believe is possible. Why would something with no meaning or purpose be wasting all this precious oxygen? No, there has to be some reason we're all in this world.

It's been my lifelong opinion (not that my life's been particularly long) that our purpose is solely to live. Since I don't believe in a necessary great being in the sky puppeteering all the little ants on the face of the earth, I have to believe in people more. We have the power to run our own lives, and we have to choose what our purpose on earth will be. That purpose, what we've done with our time alive, gives our lives, and the lives that we touch, meaning.

It doesn't take going into space or curing cancer to make a difference, to give your life or someone else's a little more meaning. A smile, an introduction, or a joke can do just as much for someone. Making the world better is a lot like quitting smoking (which in and of itself might make the world better). It requires that you take it one day, one step, at a time and that all your fellow beings support you.

It's your choice; take it one step at a time, and change the world.

— **Alison Riccardi**

When someone asks, "What is the meaning of life?" they most often mean, "What's the meaning of sentient human life?" And when you think about it, the question makes sense. A plant doesn't ask itself about the meaning of existence. It grows, moves toward the sun, reaches its roots out for water, and spreads seeds to make more of itself. There are no questions to ask. A dog is relatively content to scratch its ears, living in comfort long enough to procreate. We, however, are good at asking questions.

So when we ask what life's purpose on this green earth is, we really want to know why we can wonder why. And if we can give

ourselves a definitive purpose, explain why we can question ourselves, we can just attribute all that reproducing and ear-scratching
of the lower orders to the service of us. It fits in with religion. Hell,
it even fits in with logic. If we're the smartest and the wisest, obviously everything below us should help us out.

But then again, why are we the smartest and the wisest and
good at asking questions (assuming that we even are, and knowing
a few smart brine shrimps, I doubt it)? Why did we among all creatures earn or receive the power to recognize existence? Only we
have the power to create vast tapestries of stories and lies and lives.
As creative and as clever as a cat is, only humans created the cat god-
dess Bast. And even then, she's just a human body with a cat head.
When we draw cartoon animals, we usually toss in some anthropo-
morphic limbs or in the very least, eyes.

So what's the big deal? Why can we do all this?

I'm going to paraphrase my father and simply say the answer is
because we are. And that's the way it is. We are sentient. We exist.

As the purpose of life for plants is to create seeds and grow and
do what plants do best and the purpose of cats is to scratch and eat
and make kittens and do what cats do best, the purpose of our lives
are to just do what we do best. Our purpose is to create children's
books and bombs and two-seat bicycles and sewer systems and
babies. We're good at it; we do it a lot.

We shouldn't feel shame in doing what we do best. Because

we're able to. And, in being able to, we should. We should use our creativity to find plants and herbs and turn them into substances that provide deliciously inviting sensations. And we should find new ways to stop other people from making those plants into these drugs. We should f*** every which way, and we should also create books and theses and speeches to keep anyone from ever touching the flesh of another person. We should agree while contradicting. We should burn crosses and refuse to give up our seats on a bus. Because we can.

And I don't mean this in a nihilistic way. Or a hedonistic way. Or any form of "istic" or "ist" that our good people have created to describe ourselves and find reasons for acting the way we do. I only mean my explanation as that: an explanation. Whatever reason we create to blame ourselves for being the way we are — be it God, evolution, or any other equally meaningless and useless explanation — we are. We are human. We are life. Life must do what life does best. And we do a lot of things best.

So what is the meaning of sentient human life?

To write explanations like this.

Go and be human now.

— Mike Drucker

Life is survival.

We all have different hopes and fears, needs and desires, beliefs and superstitions, physical features and moral standards. How, with all those differences, do we manage to get through even one day without a new war or riot breaking out? The earth should be total chaos by now.

My analysis: we (people, groups, and nations) get through daily life by seeking common ground, whenever possible. By having a positive, productive, proactive slant on life, by sublimating the fear caused by our differences and by sublimating the anger and aggression that is our natural defense against that fear. This avoidance, this sublimation, is not cowardice; it is survival!

Unfortunately, these tricks, these methods, this avoidance, this sublimation does not always ensure our survival. Occasionally the only defense against annihilation is positive, brutal action — war. It hurts my peaceful soul (and I am, seriously a very peaceful guy) to say it, but some situations are too dangerous, too volatile, to avoid, ignore, or otherwise close your eyes to. I'll say no more about war — you all know what I'm talking about.

My philosophy: in general, I see radical, blind allegiance to any religion, cause, or political philosophy as one of those dangers to survival. You could assume from that statement that I go through life believing in nothing, but that would be very far from the truth. I believe in many things, and very strongly in some things, but nothing I believe is set in cement. I can, and have, changed my mind, based on logic and circumstance. Not to do so is 1) to go through life with a set of blinders on and 2) to be dangerously sure that you know everything there is to know about a subject. Personally, I don't believe that there is anyone who knows everything about any given subject, especially me.   **— Harvey Grund**

Life is faith. Life is honesty. Life is the fulfillment of dreams. Even the unwelcome failure contributes to the great joyride we call life. Life is really something taken for granted each day the sun shines or a beautiful breeze is ignored. Life, to me, is the completion of a want as well as a need to give. Life is so much more than words. Life is a single breath.   **— Crystal Mosser**

Life is an unpredictable progression of cause-and-effect relationships. Having one defined route, a formula for how our life should be lived, would make life routine and systematic. Our lives do not have scripts; rather, we write our own scripts. Following a script — a set path for life — would lead to completing life, not experiencing it.

Living means defying convention and doing what your instincts tell you to do. Living means having those moments when you cannot explain what you are doing, but following what your senses tell you to do; it means having those moments when somebody asks you what you are thinking, but you have no answer because you are living, not thinking.

We cannot find life's meaning through mere introspection. Understanding who we are, where we came from, and where we are going comes first from understanding who others are, their pasts and futures. By talking to the stranger in the elevator, the coffee shop worker, the taxicab driver, the bellman, or the person sitting next to us on the train, we see who they are by listening to how they see themselves. Then we can begin to look at who we are by listening to how we see ourselves.

But realizing that this perception of ourselves is ever-changing enriches our lives and keeps us from becoming complacent. What we think our meaning is changes as we grow, but what remains constant is our drive to experience life, cherishing it as best we can.

As George Carlin said, "Life is not measured by the number of breaths we take, but by the moments that take our breath away."

— **Phillip Hennessey**

In order:
Born. Family. Learn. Grow up. Hard work. Learn. Procreation. Family. Learn. Nurturing. Learn. Hard work. Leadership. Family. Fish.   — **David McPeak**

The meaning of life is the search for the meaning of life. The search itself is what helps us simultaneously attain wisdom and to create our own wisdom through our life experience. Searching gives us context for the lessons that result. Searching gives us reason (directly or indirectly) for waking up. It gives us a sense of unfinished business that propels us. In my opinion, if you can't look at things this way, the concept of life seems off-kilter. If we aren't searching for the meaning of life in every action that we take, then we are just looking for tasks to fill our time. It is the search for meaning that leads us to religion, or spirituality, or a rejection of those things. And "those things" are some of the most powerful forces in society.   — Jesse Lanier

My favorite movie is *Harold and Maude*. It's an unusual movie, from 1971, that at first shocked, confused, and almost horrified me. It's about an extremely wealthy and bored young man, Harold, who is fascinated by death and regularly fakes his own suicide to traumatize his mother, and an eighty-year-old woman whom he befriends, Maude, who is in love with life and always looking for a "new experience." Through their many adventures together, the two end up falling in love. The idea of a twenty-year-old sleeping with someone old enough to be his grandmother sounds icky at first, of course, but when you open your mind to the movie it's easy to realize the real message — that love has no confines, no boundaries, and that it always ultimately triumphs.

Harold and Maude also satirizes American society in the early seventies: the controversy over the Vietnam War, its obsession with psychoanalysis, its class structure, and the needless destruction of the environment. Though the movie is full of hilarious and heartfelt scenes, the one that always affects me the most comes at the very end. It is Maude's eightieth birthday, and Harold has thrown her a party. She reveals to him that she has taken pills to kill herself, and that she'll be dead in a few hours. She simply has gotten the most that she can out of life and wants to leave it before it inevitably gets worse, for she is the happiest she's ever been. Harold will not accept her choice to die and rushes her to the hospital. In the ambulance on the way there, she tells him not to be sad. He protests that he loves her, over and over. And then she delivers my favorite line in the movie, possibly my favorite line in any movie: "Oh, Harold, that's wonderful! Go and love some more."

I have never been able to hear that line without getting teary-eyed. It is at that moment that all the bizarre occurrences of the movie compile to warm your heart and reveal their true message — that love, no matter what form it takes, is always good, and that humans, in an absurd, violent, anguish-filled world, should work their whole lives to simply love as much as they can. It is, in my opinion, the most important thing in the world. If you take Maude's words, words that can make the world better, to be the meaning of life and put them into practice, your life will never cease to be fulfilling.

— Lillian Hofer

Over the years, exposure to society diluted what I felt was my unique brand of sadism, and a battle with a bad case of OCD and the pressures of trying to find my niche in the unforgiving middle-school social structure left me too exhausted to express it. From studying classics like *Oedipus Rex* and the Shakespearian tragedies, I learned when I was supposed to feel guilt and despair, and how I was supposed to express it. Though I had acquired this understanding of "how" and "when" to feel certain ways, I never truly grasped "why." It seemed to me that Oedipus bore no responsibility for his crimes, that they were results of the immutable laws of fate. Therefore he should leave Thebes for the good of the people, but leave with a clear conscience. Why he let grief over accidental, though enormous, transgressions of the taboo drive him to self-destruction was beyond me.

But, nonetheless, I mellowed out, and by high school I developed a healthy sense of compassion and became genuinely likable, and liked. Despite this partial reformation, however, I never developed a true sense of empathy, sorrow, or guilt.

So my junior year, when my friends confronted me to tell me it wasn't fair what had happened to me, to assure me that I was a "good guy," to implore me "not to let it consume me," and to offer their sympathy, I kept my gaze fixed on the floor rather than look into their terribly sympathetic eyes and let them in on the terrible secret that I didn't feel bad.

Cerebrally, of course, I knew that I had abruptly ended the life of an innocent, good woman, ruined the life of her husband, and robbed two children my age of their mother. I knew I should act guilt ridden. I had emerged from a car accident I caused that had ruined four people's lives with little more than a piece of windshield embedded in the bottom of my shoe, but in my heart I felt no different. It was as if, because I hadn't seen the motorcycle, and therefore hadn't even had the opportunity to make a decision, let alone a wrong or immoral one, I was not responsible for my actions. I slept that night, and well. I went to school the next day. Unable to explain that only my sense of decency kept me from turning this event into an excuse not to go to school — as I had let the equally untraumatic death of my dog be used as an excuse not to go to tae kwon do — I offered lamely to those who asked the "therapeutic effects of routine."

A month later, a science teacher at my high school would die because his doctor had failed to properly sew up an incision made in an ordinarily low-risk surgery, and I realized that perhaps if I had looked up, I would not have found myself looking into sympathetic eyes, but into a reflection of my own: the look of someone yearning to feel what they are not feeling. The task of memorializing Mr. Greenway fell to our school's chapter of the Science National Honor Society. We had an excess of money and plenty of precedent to work with: our school is old, and dark plaques dot the auditorium and halls commemorating those who died while students or teachers at Plant High. We held our first meeting, during which we discussed our heavy obligation and elected members to fill the club's vacant offices, but a second meeting never came, and ultimately the responsibility was forgotten amid AP exams and college applications.

Almost one year to the day later, while driving my girlfriend home from work, she received a phone call from her friend Thomas telling her that our friend Kyle Howton had died in a car accident, and I got to watch all the pain I had caused firsthand. The other driver in the accident, unfamiliar with the area, had blown a partially obscured stop sign, nicked the back of her car, and sent her hurtling into a tree.

The funeral home frantically scrambled to find seating. The chapel was packed, and five peripheral rooms were converted to standing room only, the service piped in through closed-circuit video. Many people were forced to remain outside to hold a sort of private memorial service by themselves. The streets were converted to parking lots, and a good fourth of South Tampa was shut down for the occasion. I believe it was while I was standing in that room, watching Kyle's service on the television and the tears in my friends' eyes that the tiny bit of windshield drove its way through my shoe and into my soul.

Though I did not realize it at the time, this opportunity to witness catastrophic accidents from the perspectives of both the responsible and the harmed has lent me a strong identification with personal tragedy and guilt. When hearing news of a ferry accident near Staten Island, tears well up in my eyes for those who lost friends and family, and even for those whose fault it was. Drug busts over international waters lead me to lament the children and wives losing their husbands and serve to remind me of the terrible debauchery with which their product is usually associated, leading me to more unease, and tears. And when visiting museums and staring at paintings, I can pick out Longinus from the phalanx, and recognize Socrates' executioners receding though a corridor in the background, with their hands raised in explanation and the unmistakable look of guilt in their eyes.   — Derick Vollrath

There is no one meaning of life. It is something some of us find on our own (we must give our lives meaning, through some effort) and that some are given during our upbringing (your life means X to God and, hence, to you). Many of us don't seem to grapple with it until confronted with beginnings or endings. And even then it isn't a question that occurs to every culture. Where we do find the question, posing it signifies a privileged life, in that some of one's energy is available for idle thought.

The more successful responses to this nonuniversal question, which you can reword as "how to think and feel about our aloneness," will reach beyond ourselves. Outside of living for family or within a monastic tradition, a newer answer has been "to buy stuff." I keep hoping more people will decide that social action is the best way to endow one's life with meaning. Compassion as the bridge to and through the loneliness of others makes me part of something larger than myself; any resulting action makes my existence meaningful.

— **Peter Sardellitto**

A friend asked me a while ago what the meaning of life was; I believe his exact words were, "Why are we here?" I recall that I didn't flinch or hesitate. I just blurted out, "To die. But in the meantime, to laugh."

I believe that although the test of time has taught me many things, and I want nothing more than to expand on that statement with revelations and profound notions, I must carefully remind myself that my statement served the question well and that any alteration of such a simple and powerful notion should be handled delicately.

— **Michael Stone**

A lot of people, many much wiser than me, have contemplated what life is, and more so, the meaning, if any, behind it. This humble philosopher believes the meaning does not come through life, but rather, through death. A person cannot truly be judged for his or her actions while alive; any action can be trumped by the next choice the bearer makes. It is only at death that past actions become as potent as the day they were enacted and thus steadfast. Similar to all great works of art, the truth and the meaning are not understood until the paint dries. Why should this not apply to life as well? If life were meant to have meaning, eulogies would not be reserved for the dead.
— **Marc Bauer**

Life by its very definition means "to live." The question becomes, How do we do that? Stop thinking about what you did yesterday or what you will do tomorrow, and begin paying attention to what you are doing right now. Begin to understand that what you are doing right now will create what you will do tomorrow. Life becomes meaningful only when we finally choose to live in the here and now.

Just think, if you were in the here and now, you might notice that hungry person staring at you because you have food. Or you might notice that the person over there is laughing and feeling joyful just to be alive, and instead of reacting with fear, you might just relate. I am sitting in a chair. It is hard on my butt. My hands are touching keys and making these words come forth. My dog stares up at me with nothing but pure love as my feet touch this cool surface called a floor. I love this moment. This! is the meaning of life. To have every emotion you can have and to be the grandest human being you can be in this moment. To know that everything you see and touch are only a part of you, and so to love it and respect it as you would yourself. Live each moment as if it were your last, and slide into your grave with a grin on your face going "yeeeeeeee-haaaaaaa."

                   — Susan Mcanulty

It seems like such a profound question, but it's really quite simple. The meaning of life is to leave the things on this planet better than how found them. Whether it's your family, your community, your job, or even your recreation, the ultimate goal is to make them better. If you can succeed in accomplishing just one of those tasks, you have lived a full life.

                   — Nicolle Morrison

Life is being young and in love. Crying, laughing, screaming, smiling. Life is knowing that the best is yet to come but that the worst may not be over. It's knowing every day that someone out there understands you, knowing that your smile may brighten someone's day, knowing that there are generations that lived before you and generations to come. Life is just *being*. Being a kid, being a grand-parent, being a citizen, being happy…being whatever you want.

— **Rachel**

Life seems to be a long series of situations that you can either accept and confront or ignore and move on.

An individual can choose a course that is in his or her own best interest or a course that is in the best interest of others. It is in the space between self-interest and selflessness that life occurs and is most fruitful.

By deciding to ignore a situation, you let life pass you by. At some point everyone does this, and sometimes it's the best decision you can make. Do this too often, though, and you might find your-self too far along in life with very little to show for it.

— **Michael Baird**

When all is said and done, life is as deceptive as Descartes thought it would be. Your senses fool you daily, so much that you do not know what or whom to trust. The only certainty is that you are always in the process of thinking — thus the phrase "I think, there-fore I am." Although this sounds like some kid is trying to impress you with his intellect by ripping out tidbits from a history textbook, it is in fact relevant beyond belief. This is a very abstract question that philosophers have been trying to crack for years, without a ful-filling explanation. If obligated to answer this question at gunpoint, I would say life's meaning is to explore life as much as possible, to understand why it is called a gift, to experience both pain and love — simply stated, to experience the best of both worlds.

— Evan Joseph S.

To find the meaning of life, you need to look no further than your newborn child's smile. Everything in the world disappears in that instant as, for a brief second in time, you realize life is perfect.

— Super Michael V.

Remember the 1963 movie It's a *Mad, Mad, Mad, Mad World?* A diverse group of people engage in a mad dash to discover buried treasure. Following a clue left by an old bank robber with his dying breath, they know it's in a park in Santa Rosita, California, under a "big W."

As they scurry through the park with their picks and shovels, trying to beat their rivals to the treasure, the wife of one of the treasure hunters — disgusted with the behavior of her hubby and the others, whose greed has turned them into near-savages — looks up after taking a drink from a water fountain and suddenly sees it: four palm trees, leaning at angles to each other to form a big W.

It was so big, and so out in the open, that nobody saw it. Nobody except the one person who wasn't looking for it.

The meaning of life is a lot like that. All the meditation, religion, numerology, astrology, psychology, mysticism, and psychedelic drugs will not reveal the meaning of life, because the answer is so simple, so out in the open, that you virtually have to be a disinterested observer to see that it is almost right in front of your eyes.

Everything that exists is dependent on what has gone on before. You are here because your parents were born, grew up, and had you. And their parents did the same, and so on. Your great-great-grandparents, and your great-grandparents, and your grandparents, and even your parents may all be dead now, but what they did in their lives, and what they did to shape their children's lives, shaped everything that has happened since then.

Thomas Edison invented the record player and the lightbulb, and even though he has been dead for over seventy years, the impact he made on the world has affected virtually every human being. How different would your life have been without electric light and recorded music?

In the movie *Pay It Forward*, a young boy decides that the way to improve the world is to do something nice for a stranger and to tell that stranger to show his gratitude by doing something nice for another stranger.

Now, think for a moment: After you are dead, what will be left to show that you existed? The answer: the impact you left on the world.

Did you create and give? Did you inspire others to create and give? Did you spread love? Did you raise a child who feels good about him- or herself and who will in turn raise his or her child to feel the same?

Or were you petty, mean, cheap? The kind of person nobody will miss? Did you live every day as a zero-sum game in which you felt that in order to be "ahead," others had to suffer a loss? Were you selfish, rude, a real jerk? Did you amass wealth and not use a cent of it to improve anybody else's life, or the world at large?

The meaning of life lies in how you made the world different from the way you found it. It's simple. It's real. It's obvious. It does not depend on speculation or mysticism. It does not require belief in anything that cannot be proven.

Embrace this meaning, and let it inspire you to make your legacy positive. After you are gone, the impact you have had on others will be the meaning of your life.   **— Larry Rogak**

Life is the most mysterious and celebrated state ever to be enjoyed and experienced. Life can be taken for granted, given away, spared, wasted. Life is the test given to every human being, with a clock ticking away in the background, to see what they can do with the precious few years they are given but not guaranteed. Life is the raw material of happiness, sadness, frustration, elation, and finality. Life is the insatiable mistress, demanding every day. Life is the nurturing mother, comforting the despondent to look forward to a better tomorrow. Life is the mocking crowd, jeering at the losers, and the adoring public, cheering on the winners and underdogs. Life is the sun rising, listening to the robin sing. Life is the screaming of horror, ripping through the night. Life is the sobbing over a lost one, or the ecstatic joys brought by a newborn baby. Looked at comically, the meaning of life is no parole. — **Robert R. Fitzsimmons**

I have been alive 10,983 days. I can't help but think I've wasted around 10,900 of them.

By wasted, I mean I've spent the days hidden behind a desk at the office or slept until noon or wallowed in a bad mood. I've been ill, watched too much TV, or surfed the Internet for entirely too long. There are 10,900 days I don't remember.

But I could probably recall vividly around eighty-three different days of my life. These are the days I graduated from college, adopted my dog, Lucy, got married, played my first song on the guitar, or published my first poem. They also include the day my grandfather died and the day my first boyfriend broke my heart.

The days I remember aren't all happy or pleasant; they didn't always teach me a lesson or make me a better person. But they always, always made me feel something: excitement, pride, sadness, love, exhilaration. There is an overwhelming emotion tied to each of these days that makes them impossible to disregard.

It is so easy to pass a day without having felt anything. To me, my life has meaning only when I've felt something I can't forget.

— Vicki L. Wilson

Having a meaning necessitates our being created by an entity with intelligence, and it requires that this entity created us with purpose.

Our meaning, therefore, is success in that purpose.

We must determine what we were designed for, what our mission details are. We cannot otherwise truly and objectively determine whether or not we've been, or are being, successful.

If we haven't been designed with a goal, how can we succeed? If there's no set objective, how can we attain it? How, without guidance or feedback from the creator, can we determine if we are reaching our potential or whether we're heading toward or away from success?

Without an objective understanding of our design and purpose, the definition of *success* must always be subjective. Without an intelligent creator, we are just machines with no understanding of our purpose. We attempt to succeed when we don't even know what the goal is. In lieu of an externally prescribed objective, we attempt to create our own. And if we are truly convinced that our life is without purpose, we will die.

So we must attempt to create meaning ourselves. This is the best we can possibly hope to do.   — Jinky Williams

Since none of us is an expert on the creation of the universe, because none of us created it, and none of us was alive for the past billions of years to witness it, then we can safely say that we are all just trying to make sense of it. We believe in philosophies, truths, dogmas, faiths, or sometimes the lack thereof that have been passed down to us through myriads of ways of telling.

To scrape it down to a skeletal essence, then the truth I believe in is this: to *love* others as best we possibly can and, for the sake of Pete and heaven, to love something bigger, greater, and beyond ourselves, something we did not create or have the power to create, something intangible and made holy by our very belief in it.

This is not the soaped-up, sexed-out version of love that many of us resign to. Rather, it is the kind of love that causes us to forgive those who hurt us and to risk our lives. It is not magical, or impossible, for it is within us all to love others so fiercely that in the end we could give it all up. This scary notion cuts much deeper than any hurt we experience or inflict, because it is buried under layers of silliness, sadness, pain, fear, and American dreams.

This is all easy to say, hard to do, but worth every effort we can muster.   — **Barbra Bowman**

I've always been a very outgoing person. I love to meet people, talk to them, find out where they're from, what they do, who they know, why they're here, what motivates them, what inspires them.

When I'm on the train going to or from work, I don't hesitate to strike up a conversation with the stranger sitting next to me. And more often than not, that stranger is more than happy to talk about ... well, whatever he or she wants to talk about. Sometimes, we don't even exchange names, but it doesn't matter. After a while, that person is no longer a stranger to me, nor I to them.

A few weeks ago, I took the morning train and perused the crowded car. I noticed the "regulars," the people who take the same train every day and sit in the same car — even the same seat. I noticed the girl who sits in the back corner of the car with her knees up on the seat in front of her, sleeping with her black hood pulled over her head. I saw the same gray-haired old man with the tattered, brown briefcase who calls his wife on his cell phone every morning as the train passes Bridgeport. I also noticed, for the first time, a very tall, thin black man standing by the doors of the car. The train was crowded, and he couldn't find a seat. He wore a tired, sullen look, and I couldn't help but feel for him. Eventually, he found a seat and rested.

That same evening, I worked late and got to the station around 7:30 — about fifteen minutes before my train was scheduled to arrive. The platform was deserted, save one person: the man I had seen on the train that morning. I bought my ticket at the automated ticket-vending machine and stood next to the bench where he was sitting.

"I hate working late on Fridays," I said casually.

"I know what you mean — I'm on my way to work right now," the man responded, chuckling.

And so the ice was broken, and we talked. His name was Chidi. He was from Nigeria. He had just moved to the United States a month earlier to be with his mother and brothers, who had moved to New York six years prior. His English was impeccable, and he bore a slight British accent.

Our train arrived, and we sat next to each other and continued to talk about everything from college to music to work to life in the States to life in Nigeria. I learned more about Nigeria in forty-five minutes than I had known in my entire life. Chidi told me about his college years and the influence that Tupac and Biggie had on him and his friends.

"Nigerians listen to Tupac?" I thought to myself. I was astounded.

Finally, we arrived at my stop. I shook hands with my new friend and went home.

This morning, for the first time in almost a month, I saw Chidi again on the train. When he saw me, his eyes lit up. He remembered my face and my name, and I remembered his. We spoke briefly because it was near the end of the train ride. But it was just enough time to exchange the normal pleasantries, "What's new? How's the job? Did you find a place to live? How is your mom? Your brothers?"

It's amazing how sometimes even the most benign, run-of-the-mill conversations can make you smile and can serve as a bright spot in an otherwise bland day, especially when those conversations are with a complete "stranger."

A friend of mine has repeatedly expressed to me how amazed she is that I can talk to just about anyone. She seems to think of it as a gift, but I think she's wrong. I look at it as simply letting go of your fears and insecurities and understanding that we're all human. Once you acknowledge and embrace that commonality, the rest is easy.

I encourage everyone to try this. Start a conversation. Make a friend. Take a leap. You might be surprised by whom you meet. You may find that the person you're talking to likes the same music, has a friend that went to the same college as you, or grew up in the town next to your hometown. You may find out that the person is a complete lunatic and you may have to run...fast! You may find out that the person is as beautiful inside as they are outside — and you might get their phone number! Or you may find out that the person you're talking to is your old friend's cousin, which may then prompt you to get in touch with that old friend just in time to pay them your last respects before they pass away from terminal cancer.

— **Andrew Schmidt**

The meaning of life is simply to have sex, have children, and continue the big picture. Not everyone is a genius inventor. The best you can do is have some children and hope that somewhere down the line you have led to someone great.   — **Steve Dusome**

The point isn't to keep from making mistakes. It's how you handle those mistakes that defines your life.   — **Ben Violette**

I think the meaning lies in the joy of discovering that our separateness is an artificial boundary we construct.

By becoming selfless, we are freed to incredible happiness.

But stash some reserves for yourself in a plan B in case the selfless thing doesn't work out.   — **Mike Dayoub**

The meaning of life is never-ending. It continues even once you have said your last good-byes to sight sound, taste, and feelings.

The meaning of life is to be a creator. We are the creation of the Great Spirit Creator, and we are created to be just that. This universe is ours. This is our domain. All we need to do is provide and maintain.

The meaning of life is giving words to that which you wish to obtain. We are all learning lessons as souls on different levels, just as if we were in school. Going through this, surviving that, building character for the next time you are sent back. You will either pass or fail. Thus you are simply creating your own heaven and your very own hell. Peace.   **— Najmah Ebony Omega**

I am a simple woman with a complex emotional irrationality. Can my words even matter here? Probably not.

But what if they did?

What if I come up with something that really touches someone? What if I come up with something that changes the way someone views their life altogether? What if the words I type now influence someone, and what if that influence carries on for generations of that person's family? I could quite literally change the world. Right here, right now.

That's some serious pressure. I don't know if I'm up to it. I don't know if I can handle that kind of responsibility.

But you know what? Somewhere, at some time, some total stranger's words changed the way I saw my life. In fact, it happens all the time, doesn't it?

What is the meaning of life? I believe it is knowing that your words and ideas are powerful, and that they *can* make a difference. Maybe to someone, maybe to something, maybe somehow.

So what do we do with that?

Never, ever forget it.

Your words and ideas have the ability to help someone expand and grow and live and breathe and experience in a whole new way!

Imagine, a whole world full of people who are living and experiencing *truly* — just because of something you said.

Keep talking, keep writing, keep dreaming.

You owe it to the world.

— R. Lindsay

I might say that the meaning of life is a hard day's work and a beer in the hand when I get home. Or I might say the meaning of life is the feeling you get after the first time you have an orgasm brought on by someone other than yourself. I also could say that it is the moment when you find your soul mate or "true love" and your eyes meet for the first time. All these scenarios could be interpreted as the meaning of life. However, I say the meaning of life is when you fall down the first time and no one is watching, and you pick yourself up, dust yourself off, and check to see if anyone saw, and carry on with whatever you were doing in the first place. That's the meaning of life, because life has a lot of little snags that might trip you up, but it is up to you to assess the damage, minimize the embarrassment, and keep moving on to the next challenge. Keep on living: that's what is most important.   — **Jeannie Sallis**

Life is a journey. Some of us journey through many years, and sadly, some of us have a few minutes in which to experience life. Some of us are fortunate enough to find a place where we belong, and some of us search for a place to call home. Some of us may never find it.

Life is choice. Some people don't have many choices to make, and some struggle through daily trials. We can choose to make our own or someone else's life better through our actions. Some people choose not to.

Life is wonderful. We must make life better for all by respecting, acknowledging, and helping each other along the way.

Life is a great mystery. We may never know "why we are here" or "what is the meaning of life," so we shouldn't spend our time thinking about it when there is so much to experience.

Life is everywhere. It is all around us. Cherish life and all it has to offer.   — **Trevor Dysart**

Finding a meaning to life is itself the meaning of life. This quest for spiritual truth is what makes us human and differentiates us from the rest of the animal kingdom. Humans are the only animals to ask "why," the only animals to wonder where we came from, what we are, and where we're going. Finding a purpose or a passion, whether it be religious faith, love, or simply a hobby, is a uniquely human ability. Life is our only opportunity to embrace this privilege. Unfortunately, so many religions and belief systems encourage the opposite idea — that this mortal existence is merely a test or preparation for what lies beyond death. But life is no dress rehearsal. This is the time to explore, to indulge our curiosity and our hunger for truth.   — **Tracy Steel**

We cannot all climb to the top of the great mountain to consult with the guru about life's meaning. Those of us with fewer means and less fitness must work it out here at sea level. I think when we are young we believe the meaning of life lies in how it satisfies us.

As we grow we extend our network and learn that meaning comes from satisfying others, looking to and out for others. That implies action. I guess, unlike the guru, I do not wish to sit and contemplate my navel. I think actions are very important. Making those phone calls or buying something special for someone or crossing the street to see why that person is crying. The Beatles probably said it better than the gurus: "All you need is love," and the love you need is the love you have to give. It is better to love than to be loved. But usually giving implies receiving too. **— Christine Emmert**

Being human is about not being satisfied with anything. And most of the time, that totally sucks. We want to just be happy with what we have, but if that were the case, we'd all be dead in the water. And so instead we fantasize and dream. We always look to change something, to go somewhere, to be different in some way. We can never rest, because as soon as we slow down, as soon as we stop caring about bigger and better things, we die. The meaning of life is perpetual motion to get to some higher point. As soon as we reach what we think is the peak, we realize we still have a long way to go. That might be frustrating, but it's also fun.   **— Ruvym Gilman**

We are given, at max, a century to experience everything this world has to offer. We are all given different opportunities, different capabilities, and different societies to battle or integrate into. But each of us is given a chance — to placidly sit by and watch others live, or to live as if no one was watching.   — **Kennon Hulett**

I do not know the "meaning of life," only that it can be lived better or worse. I have the power to make that decision. My grandma used to tell my mom that for every door that closes, a window opens. My mom now tells me that. I have made decisions I'm not proud of, but I made them and stuck by them. I am happy right now, but only because a few doors slammed and some windows let some fresh air in. If it wasn't for a failed marriage, I wouldn't have moved on and ended up in an even worse relationship. It was bad at the time, but I see now that it was leading somewhere else. I learned about myself and what I wanted and, most important, that no one could make me happy but me. Until I learned that, I couldn't move on. It's hard work growing up!

Now, at thirty-one, I've found a wonderful person and a life that suits me because I'm happy within. I believe in myself and trust that even though I cannot make sense of things sometimes as a door closes, another window will open to give me a view of a different path. Things will work out, maybe not as I planned, but when I look back, I know I will be where I am supposed to be. I find great comfort in knowing that.   — **Tina Schmitt**

Life is about beauty, passion, nature, and the little things, such as the way little fizzies magically appear when you open a can of soda, or the way you jump out of your seat when your favorite hockey team scores a magnificent goal. But it's not just about fun, fun, fun. Passion means pain, work, and suffering. We all hope to never again experience the heartache of our first breakup or the first passing of a loved one. But while the pain may have borne a hole in our hearts at the time, it left a scar — superficial yet lingering — that reminds us of all the things that led up to the heartache, good and bad, and what we learned from them.

Life is about feeling. Some people look to create magic through their work with science or their daily prayers. What they don't understand is that life is magic and those things they toil away at are just part of the ride. Everything from the way a single leaf floats down from a tree to absorbing the splintering pain when you sprain your ankle to the warm greetings of your beloved canine companion — it's all part of life, for better or worse. When you become numb — socially, emotionally, or physically — you've lost touch with life. When you can no longer experience laughter and hurt, when you become a slave to the day-to-day grind, when you *just don't care* anymore, that's when you lose touch.

Life is about not giving up when things get too hard. It is about remembering to absorb every moment of a wonderful event.

The meaning of life is laying on your deathbed and saying, "I had no regrets."
— **Mike Chen**

When people argue against the existence of God, they often say, "I just can't believe in a God that allows so many terrible things to happen in the world." And looking around it's easy to see what they mean. Headlines inform us daily of mass murders, school bus crashes, suicide bombers. It's so easy to ask, "Why couldn't God have just stopped that suicide bomber?" "Why couldn't God have just saved those children?" "Why couldn't Hitler have had an aneurysm at seventeen, sparing millions of lives?"

But I don't think we can live in a world without suffering. If no one suffered, then all people would have to be perfect all the time. Without the ability to cause suffering, we lose the ability to choose. Life is ultimately a choice, of how you will live, what you will do, what you will say, what you will believe. We could have been made to be all good, all the time. But we would have no choices, and to choose to be good is worth infinitely more than the most saintly goodness of a choiceless robot.

Many people believe we are born with a soul. I believe that our soul is the product of an entire life; it's something you make. It's shaped by how often you are kind to others, by how you treat your children, by how hard you work for the things you care about. Life is a dazzling and confusing array of choices, and what you do makes you who you are. We may begin life with different personalities and different situations, but what matters is not what we start with but what we end with, and how we confront everything in between. Every religion, at its core, gives us advice on the best way to live, but in the end it's a choice we make only for ourselves. We may choose to feed the starving or to kill the innocent, but no matter what our earthly rewards or punishments may be, every action we take makes us who we are. And what, at last, could be more precious than the quality of our own character, and the integrity of our soul?

— Julia Darcey

If there is some cosmic meaning I think it's improbable that anyone will ever discover it. How would one even start? There are so many possibilities. Who says a cosmic meaning has to have anything to do with human beings? Let's say it has to do with some intelligent beings in a galaxy a billion light-years away. How could you ever make that connection? I don't think there's any value in investigating any further.

As for a personal meaning of life: live long and prosper.

— Ian Smith

Life could be so much better if people were taught to think critically during their childhoods. So many people live by reacting, because they don't know how to put two and two together. This makes life more difficult for those of us who try to formulate sustainable reasons before doing something, because we usually end up fixing what they've broken. Think of all the crimes, wars, and other catastrophes that could be prevented if people just remembered that their actions have consequences.   — **Lauri Apple**

Why do we exist? I like to think it's those little moments we carry with us always: a perfect sunset, the first time you know you're in love, owning your first car, your wedding day, the birth of your children. It's these snapshots of time that drive us ever onward.

— **Geoffrey Blake**

Choose the meaning of life from one of the four listed below:

1) Life has no intrinsic meaning beyond what we attribute to it. Our task is to infuse our lives with whatever meaning will ensure we stay with it to the end.

2) The meaning of life is way beyond our grasp. Naturally, we do our best to grasp it, but it is essentially ungraspable.

Our life is a continual process of seeking that meaning, and living in the heart of that seeking. When we stop seeking we have either given up on it or decided that we have it figured out. In either case we are wrong, and life begins to die from there.

3) Life means love. Our lives are treasure hunts for love. When you find the treasure, you find yourself; you are love, you are life, you live.

4) Life is an experiment. Can we bear to live without meaning? If we can live without meaning, we will be destroyed. If we cannot live without meaning, we will destroy ourselves. If we find meaning, we will fight to live. If enough people find enough meaning, humankind will live. If a critical mass does not find meaning soon enough, the experiment will be complete, and humankind will be gone.

— **Wend Stewart**

I sat down in the unemployment office contemplating the meaning of my miserable existence. Damn, I wished I had some money or a job. I looked out the window and saw a jacket-and-tie man drive by in a Benz...smiling. Well, back to my job search. Was it really all about the money? No, my college degree taught me more than that. Yet still the philosophies of Mill and Kant offered me little help in my time of need. I'm into the nonprofit thing, but I just can't get a job. Maybe I'll just sell my soul. Be a stripper or something. That pays a lot. Or better yet, an investment banker. (Like they'd hire my unshaven ass.) Why did I not just end my life then? Ha, that was a crazy thought. And never see my love again? I knew she loved me, no matter how broke I was. And at least my mother loved me too. I could not give up the beach, the trees. Sometimes when humankind gets me down I just want to talk to an animal. They never judge me. Or maybe play with a little kid who is not yet corrupted by this world. There's just too much to live for. You see, life is about love. People only complicate it. And money can buy some happiness, but the rich man is not always happy. The person who is loved and loving will always be content.

— **Reuben Albo**

Personally, I feel that the meaning of life is different for everyone. For me, the meaning of life has always been to garner knowledge. We all gain many experiences, and it's our job to analyze and learn from them. The purpose of my life is to have as many experiences as possible, whether they're good or bad. I've found that you learn more from bad experiences than you do from good ones; however, you need good ones for balance, to prove to you that life is worth living.

— **Dominique Chatterjee**

The meaning of life is best discovered when one is not thinking about what meaning life might have. A friend's warm embrace, a rack of lamb with a rosemary crust, joyfully dancing to salsa music, windsurfing off the coast of Hawaii, a brand new pair of thick comfortable socks in the winter — all these help us to experience the meaning of life.

Mercury looks lovely on an ebony countertop yet always evades your grasp if you insist on trying to touch it. So it is with the meaning of life. You know it's there, and that fact is beautiful, but to insist on pegging it down is foolhardy.

If by writing these words I help others to experience the meaning of life, and to enjoy that experience, then my own life will have acquired more meaning. Fortified with that extra meaning, tomorrow I shall breakfast not on a dull, vitamin-enhanced cereal, but rather on hot chocolate spiked with espresso, and a ham steak topped with fresh pineapple.

— **Scott Rose**

You are a blank page. When you are ready to die, you are a full-length novel.

— **Jihan Zubi**

People don't live forever, but everyone leaves their mark, which lasts eternally on those they have touched. Although the passing of our lives seems timeless, the light is slowly dimming, and one day the only thing left will be memories of what once was. That is why I choose to be the best person I can be for others, because I know that one day the only thing left of me will be the outcome of my life and how it has affected others.   **— George Montroukas**

I have no idea what the meaning of life is. It almost seems silly to think of it that way. As if it were something that could be encapsulated by one word, or one cosmology. Life is about living, and to me, each life has various meanings — determined after the fact. Life is lived in the now. No matter how much of the then and the after we carry with us as baggage, we can only be here now.

How can life be made better?

Well, now, that is a different story. In fact, telling yourself the right stories can make life better immediately. I was so sad to watch a group of complex and lovely women on one of those "reality" TV shows all repeating that when they went to the mirror they always thought bad things and told themselves about all their flaws and failures. What a terrible story to tell yourself. I look in the mirror and wiggle my eyebrows and tell myself how hot I look. Instead of telling yourself how sad you are that you don't have something, tell yourself the story of what you do have. Instead of telling yourself the story of how many things you did wrong today, tell yourself the story of all the things you did right. Did you help someone out in some way? Did you hold your tongue or your temper to spare others? Did you share a meal with others? Did you compliment someone and see them truly smile for the first time in your presence? Focus on these positive stories, and you will find yourself spending your days doing things that would make you proud of yourself.

Life can also be made better if we want less and do more. I once met these really cool raver kids who had started their own multimedia studio. We toured their studio. It was impressive. Much of it was do-it-yourself jury-rigging, but it worked and so did they. There was a sense in every room of things being accomplished. They showed me a pilot for a TV program they were prepped to show around to stations, played me tracks from CDs they were recording, and introduced me to bits and pieces of all kinds of things they were doing for the Web. When we were talking they said things like, "We could have saved up and gotten cars, but we decided to save up so we could spend our time with our friends doing cool things" and, "Now we can share what we have with our communities" and, "Some people always tell you stories of what they're gonna do; we prefer to tell people cool stories of all the things we've done, but we most especially love to talk about what we're *doing!*" They all seemed so happy and expectant and yet so relaxed. They were sure it would all work out, whatever "it" ended up being.

Be aware of your impact on the world. Notice how much you

consume and why. Do you need that thing, or are you filling an emptiness with stuff? When you stumble through the world do you leave a wake of wreckage behind?

Sharing makes life better. Trying to be content with life as it is makes life better. Doing things to make life better for others makes life better for me.   — **Robin Hand**

Change, plain and simple. Life's meaning is that everything is changing all the time.   — **Carey S. Scott**

The meaning of life can be summed up by the "thump…thump… thump" you get on the end of a fishing rod when a bass picks up your bait. It's difficult to explain or describe, but after your first experience, you understand why others spend thousands upon thousands of dollars and countless hours pursuing such quarry. At that point you are addicted. The feeling is both physical sensation and mental perception rolled into one instantaneous, fleeting event. For me, it's irrelevant if the fish is actually caught. I live for the "thump…thump…thump."   — **John N. Heutz**

We spend entirely too much time looking outside ourselves for meaning, for happiness, for gratification, for validation, or for anything we seek. The trick is to find all these things within first. Once we do that, we find affirmation of all those things in the world around us.

— Sjan Evardsson

The meaning of life is to find out if you really existed, not only as a figment of someone else's imagination.   — Matthew J. Tomczak

Every morning when I wake up, the meaning of life seems slightly different. I am not sure whether that is because each day I am slightly closer to the end of it, or whether with age I simply become more philosophical. Probably both.

There are obviously many factors involved. A new goal gives life new meaning. A new achievement puts a new perspective on it. A loss makes it suddenly seem much more precious.

This year began badly. One day I woke up and started having seizures. They got worse and worse. It looked like a brain tumor, but turned out to be epilepsy. Serious epilepsy. Now I am on medication for the rest of my life. It makes me clumsy. It makes me forget things. It makes me throw up. I felt for a while that perhaps life had no meaning at all. Perhaps we just bowl through it — with random events striking us along the way. So much of life didn't seem fair. I spent so much time contemplating the meaning of life that I started to get bogged down in thinking. I suddenly realized I was forgetting to do much actual living. Now I realize this was a great year. It was the year I didn't get a brain tumor.

I started living again. I started running to work every morning and looking at the things around me. I started running with my head up, not worrying about falling over. I started spending the time I used to spend contemplating the meaning of life thinking about things I can do to make mine good. I started thinking about the people around me — friends and family. Without thinking at all, I realized that for me, that is the meaning of my life: the people who love me.

If everyone truly treated others as they would be treated, life would be a whole lot better for all of us. It is such a simple solution, but one that so many people fail to comprehend.

The indigenous people of my country — the Maori — say it best. *Te tangata, te tangata, te tangata.* The people, the people, the people.

— **Sarah Hawk**

Just possessing a theory of some sort may only be a part of the answer. No single answer can actually be incorrect. Since we are speaking of the meaning of life, we must include the topic of creation. The creation of reality is not subject to direct destiny. Creation of reality is merely the *path* to one's destiny. Choice itself will be made sooner or later... for that choice is just a consideration of time. Your journey itself will create your desired destiny, which could be locked away inside until realization and awareness cross your path. The more we are consciously aware of what we bring to ourselves each day, the less time we spend learning through subconscious mishap upon mishap. As we progress, we begin to understand another age-old paradigm: "The more we know, the less we actually seem to know." Questions are not always given a single answer, and this question is no different. We are the artists of humanity painting on our canvas every second we live. The more we can see what we paint, the more we know what colors and strokes to use.   — Robin J. Brown

It can be made better by improving the lives of those around you. Share what you have whenever you can, ask for help when you need it, don't be afraid to be yourself.

Live simply, live honestly, live so that others emulating you are helping things too.   — Theodore John Sawchuck II

Letting go! If my fifty-one years on this earth have shown me nothing else, it's that life is really all about letting go of something, so do yourself a favor and learn how to deal with the pain, so you can "just do it."   — Marilyn Jaskolski

The human concept of God has replaced the human connection with what the Chinese refer to as *chi*, or life force. As we constantly strive for rational satisfaction, we neglect the energy and balance within the body. Our reliance on the external to guide our senses and behavior has dulled our conscious energy receptors. We are distracted by the absurd configuration of existence and so have diminished our internal balance.

The idea of God functions to create the illusion of balance within the human "soul." It gives a spiritual answer to the question of what our purpose is in living. That question has itself arisen from the crumbling of the one life into the individualized many. A "soul" is life. At birth we are given the spark of life, our little chunk of energy, that we cultivate through experience until death. Individuality gives a soul to that little chunk of life, but it is trapped within the domain of the body, and with the death of the individual dies the spark and the soul, while the energy of life is returned to whence it came. **— Mogue Rosemary**

You create your own meaning of life. It means what you want it to. There is no one set response to the question, "Why we are here?" We're not here for a reason — we're here as the result of a series of events. So if someone asks me, "What is the meaning of life?" I respond this way: "I want to live contentedly, I want the same for my son and those I care about, and so I do what I can to make that happen. Along the way I like to have fun."   — **Steve Villeneuve**

The meaning of life is a platter of BBQ ribs, coleslaw, beans, cornbread, and a tall glass of strawberry Kool-Aid. All muss, all fuss, and totally worth it.   — **Chenda Peach Ngak**

I don't know. Isn't that the point?   — **Mark Chadwick**

I wore sandals, a tank top, and shorts; my hair was damp, messily thrown up in a bun. I walked briskly down the dusty path with the golden grass tall on either side and Alexa, Paige, and Sammy in front of me. We had made it, it was summer. It was the perfect time, early evening. The sun was just beginning to set on a cloudless blue sky. I was happy. Summer is more than a season; it's more than spring, fall, or winter; it's a feeling, a way to view the world, a sense of freedom, the conjunction of carefreeness, restlessness, and recklessness. I was sixteen and balancing responsibility and privilege but leaning toward the side of too much privilege and not enough responsibility.

The narrow path widened to a small clearing with a large boulder in the middle of it. We got to the rock and sat, just waiting, waiting for something to happen. We were too early for the sunset but just in time to feel that it was actually summer. The sky there was just as carefree, restless, and reckless as we were. There is something about the sky, and there's something about being sixteen, caught in limbo between being a kid and being a young adult. And there's something that changes in the mentality of a sixteen-year-old after the last class on the last day of sophomore year.

That summer feeling kicked in right then, in that moment, and we lost interest in the stationary rock and stagnant scenery, and lost the patience to wait for the sun to set. So we left, Alexa driving, which is where reckless came crashing into carefree and restless: too carefree to mind the honking and quick accelerations on winding roads and too restless to not get in that blue sedan. We drove around aimlessly, listening to music, and as the night fell the summer moon and stars proved to be just as magical as the daytime sky. In the summer it doesn't matter what time of day it is, who you are with, what you are doing, or if you doing anything at all. The sky is always there, the one constant in life. No matter how much we all change, it remains the same, because you can never have too much sky.

— Libby Rader

Simply put: it's creating. Your gift to the world and the others around you is what you create.   — Jerry Vrabel

Each being is a blossom on the tree of life. The tree's roots stretch around the world, and its branches reach beyond our grasp of reality. If each of us can bloom in a unique shade and hue with an equally distinct fragrance, we will help our tree, our life source, to expand and grow. Our colors and essence will remain with the tree of life, revealing themselves in small doses, adding flavor and brilliance for time everlasting.   — Melissa Belgara

It blows my mind the
way some people behave.
The idea of being a "grown-up"
becomes blurred by the mind-set
that status is what makes you an adult.
There is *no* truth in this matter.
I may only be thirty-one,
sitting on the cusp of thirty-two,
still young,
but my mind and soul feel aged beyond
these people that stand before me.
My eyes have seen the birth and death of many things,

in every sense of the words *birth* and *death*.
At face value,
I may seem young,
naive,
but do the trees bow down for everyone?
Can these people feel the energy that seeps
from Nature upon touch?
These are the secrets of Ancientness.
The source of wisdom where "old age" rests.
Time gets older, life much simpler
and the soul grows brighter each day.
I have met the Elements face to face,
I know the Ancient Ones by their names
and when the wind blows,
they whisper in my ear.   **— Leonardo Minjarez**

The meaning of life is that there is no one meaning to life. We make our own meaning as we grow older. The meaning of our life is made up from our life experiences, either direct ones or someone else's. Because the world is so complex the meaning of people's lives becomes complex with their vast differences in influence. Each person's true meaning is both internal and external. The meaning comes from how these interact with each other. Beware of both aspects of your world, how they interact, and keep an open mind.   — **Steven Hambright**

Some folks search for love all their lives and never find it. Some run into it in their teens and others when they're seventy. Some strike it rich with their first love, and others with their second marriage. For me, the third time around was the lucky charm.

The younger my age, the more certain I was about the mystery of relationships. When I was a teenager, I used to think I knew everything about love and what it means. I thought I was wise to love's ways. I believed that "when we fell in love we just knew it." If it didn't work out, then it wasn't "meant to be." Such were the awe-inspiring depths of my young perceptions. As I've aged and traveled the many roads of partnership, my previous certainties and simplifications have been blown away by the winds of experience. Now I know that I know very little, if anything at all.

— **Gabriel Constans**

The meaning of life is simply put: hard lessons. Each of us must learn them every day. After all these lessons are learned, we move on to the next level of being. We hope we have learned and made the needed changes so that we do not end up repeating the difficult lessons again.

Life is really a lesson that teaches us everything we came here to learn. Many have short lessons; they only came here to teach others hard lessons. Many have lessons we all get to watch them learn. The meaning of life is to learn.   — **Ariel**

Life is a gift. There is an old Tibetan story of a blind turtle dwelling at the bottom of the ocean. Once every thousand years the turtle swims to the surface to take a breath of air. If a wooden ring were floating on the ocean, the probability that the blind turtle would surface at the exact place and put his head through that ring is the same probability that a soul will take human birth. Life is a precious, precious gift.

After fifty years I have come to understand that my life is truly in my own hands. I spent the first forty-five years in fear of being abandoned. I am now choosing faith over fear. That means taking risks to reach out to people because I believe in their essential goodness. In many ways it seems as though there is only one of us here. The meaning of my life is the discovery of this truth.

— **Vicki Danko**

The basic meaning of life, in my opinion, is just to exist for as long as we can. And we should either believe or act in such a way so that we live this time to its greatest potential. To accomplish this, we should understand that there is nothing sacred that cannot be understood or questioned. A little bit of moderation and a sense of humor never hurt anyone, either.   — **David Raymond Voth**

Awareness seems to come about in many stages. It is hard to put into words a concise meaning to the here and now. I've learned as I age to enjoy the people, places, and things I experience in this particular universe — even the bad ones. I've become an observer of how others live and interact with me and my known reality. As I know more, I've begin to experience butterflies of excitement when I think about the future, here and in the afterlife. I have always been curious, and when I met my wife, it confirmed my suspicions that life has its value in my consciousness. I hope that wherever I go, my wife will be there to join me in this sacred world. I've had too many experiences not easily explained by science or religion to expect anything less than the extraordinary.

The first night with my wife has defined me. I have had dreams that told me the future in its secret language. I have been a tree. I have talked to animals. I have seen colors that no one else saw. I know things I can't explain. My plants sing to me. Instead of allowing soulless science to explain it away like an aberration, or letting religion demonize my experiences, I accept them and keep them for my own, like a keepsake in my spiritual closet until I find someone who is capable of sharing them with me. These are what make life better.

My time spent in nature opened a discourse of the universe to me, and I expanded in my consciousness and knowing. The web of knowledge allows me to interact with all things known and unknown. And just as a mistake makes one wise, the wisdom I gather, asleep and awake, makes me a better person inside and out. By accepting these events, I also create new avenues to explore and create new openings to experience. Mundane or exciting, it is more of life, and I conjoin with it. Anyone who does anything — carpentry, music, arts and crafts, politics, swimming — learns that the better you get at it the more you do it. So it seems with my life. The more I practice, the more I enjoy it and can do it, and the more beautiful it becomes.

— **Gray Byrd**

He comes out with great exertion and pain, sliding into his father's hands. The midwife puts him on my now-flaccid stomach and I touch his waxy, plump skin. His head is covered with pale fuzz, and his eyes are squeezed shut. His dad is laughing through tears, the midwife is sewing me up, and time is frozen in this instant.

It's four A.M., and he has latched onto my breast. His dad surrounds us in his arms. I am about to fall asleep when my new baby reaches his little hand up to touch my breast. I try not to breathe. He opens up those eyes and stares one million miles into mine.

What was the question again?   **— Mary Elizabeth Shannon**

Always be nice to everyone you meet; the more friends you have the better your life will be. Always make sure that you *listen* more than you speak; too many people think that their views are right and that everyone else is wrong. Make up your own mind, and don't be hurt by what people say; after all they're only words. Life is too short to worry about what others think. Most important, *laugh every day*. Make sure that when you go to bed every night you have told the ones you love how much they mean to you.

— Jeff Rooke

To me life is never understood. It doesn't have a universal meaning or even the same meaning every day.

I've woken up tired, depressed, sad, and sometimes I've given in to self-pity and bad behavior. On those days life means nothing.

Other days I've woken up happy, full of energy and ideas for the day. On those days life means pure happiness and joy, like the sunshine.

Other days life is gray, or dumb, or busy, or sad.

Life is just everything. It does not have meaning: it's just there for you as a gift to use as you like. You can be a star one day, and a thief another, and a teacher, or a madman, or a shame, or a sunshine.

It means nothing; it's a gift.   — **Carlos Perez Chavez**

Don't look to the intellect for the answers. Life's meaning becomes known the instant you cease asking the question. Or more precisely, the answer is the dropping of the need to ask the question.

Without the question being asked, the search ends, and your body will relax and you will *feel* more alive. That's the meaning of life: to feel alive and to become more and more cognizant of the connectedness of all things.   — **Michael Alperstein**

Does life have a meaning? I think that if we all spent as much time living our lives as we spent trying to define them, we might actually live them. But of course, we are all stricken with this bizarre, DNA-encoded need to know "what it's all about." Well, what if it's about nothing? What if it's about everything? What if the Christians are right? What if the Buddhists are? Or even more interesting, what if it's the Mormons, or the Jehovah's Witnesses, or what if it's David Koresh? What if its Dr. Bronner's magical all-one hemp oil soap? The facts are simply that we'll never know. It's all an esoteric and largely irrelevant discussion that exists within the present discourse, but it's all trapped under the lid of the discourse itself, because you can never know what you don't know. It's the eternal conundrum recycled ad nauseam: What is the meaning of life? Which came first, the chicken or the egg? What is love? What is the air-speed velocity of the European swallow? Where are my car keys? Who is God? Why are we here? While we try again and again to ascertain the meaning of life, what we actually do is pontificate on what we know and try to imagine what we don't.

For my part, this is what I know: we are born into confusion, grow up in chaos, live by profit margins, and die by degrees. I hope we have some really interesting story to learn when we die, about what it was all for. I hope someone meets me on the other side and lets me ask questions until I'm satisfied. I hope that Shirley MacLaine is right, to be honest, because hers in the most interesting story I have heard yet. But until that day comes, and I either know or stop caring, I will have to be satisfied with the journey itself. There are no ends, only means. The meaning of life is the living of it. Anyone who says they have the answers is probably charging for the information.   **— Quetta Carpenter**

The day will come when you realize that you have been allotted a finite number of events to occur around you. Perhaps you will walk by the mirror in the bathroom or the nearest window or a puddle on the road, and look at your reflection for a minute. From that point on, every now and again you will be walking alone, see your reflection, and remember that cataclysmic moment. Life will become the urgency of filling up the space in between these times you remember. "Look, I've gotten this much done," you'll report back to your reflection. "I've seen the sun rise this many times. I saw a shooting star. Today I saw someone with beautiful eyes; yesterday I learned how to (un)make a friend." One day, you will see your reflection one last time and note that you have done all you needed to do. This reflection, unlike the others, will be on the inside of your eyelids.   **— Dean Gardner**

Nothing adds to quality of life like setting and achieving goals, no matter how small.   **— Roy A. Givens III**

The meaning of life? I wish I knew. How could it be made better, even? I could tell you what I think, but I'm not sure that would do us any good either. See, it seems to me that when people start talking about how to make life better, they start talking about how to make life easier, and that's not the same thing.

I'm not an old man, but I've done a few different things in my life, some of them easy and some of them hard. At one point, I had a job, a good job, that I could have kept for a long time. I was pretty good at it, and it paid pretty well. I knew the people, and they were okay. But there was one problem: it was easy, too easy, and it paid too much. So one day I quit to make my life better. I threw myself into a bad economy and an uncertain future, just to see how and what I would do.

I know what you're thinking — this guy is nuts. But I'm not. I learned a lot from doing that, and even though I'm in more debt now, and maybe I don't have a job right now, I learned a lot about what it takes to make my life good. I learned a lot about what it takes to make me happy, what it takes to keep the little wheels in my head turning, and even about security, that soft furry blanket that was putting me to sleep. A lot of times I miss that blanket, but all in all, taking the leap was the best thing I ever did. I could have sat at that desk for a long time, and I wouldn't have figured out thing one about myself or the real meaning of my life.

So I guess that's my answer — go out and find it. I can't tell you what the meaning of your life is — hell, I can't even really tell you about mine. But I've got faith in you. Sit down, look in the mirror, have a cigarette or some tea or whatever you do, and ask yourself if you're doing what you want to, or if you're just too afraid to change. Figure out what you really want to do. Then take a chance and go out and do it. It might be hard at first, but I'm sure you'll get the hang of it.

— Ethan Hartman

The meaning of life is cobwebby to a spider, running in circles to the caged hamster, chocolate chip cookies to a toddler who needs to feel better, even if there is a monster in the closet.

We pray for the right answer, the best one out of three. We desperately need to believe life is not a crapshoot, that we didn't get tossed out into a biological soup just to tickle someone's fancy. Ah, but what if that's a part of the meaning? What if life's a game and we're all "it"? What if life's about how we act while we're "it"?

I'm it, therefore I am!

Could it be that simple?   — **Patricia Galbraith**

Life is all about ass. No, really!

You spend your entire life busting it or trying to cover it up, so you don't get caught kissing it or kicking it. If you're good enough to get away with it, you end up laughing it off because you're actually able to get a piece of it. Well, as long as you're not being one!

— **HockeyGod**

Death, War, Greed, Hate, Finance, Cancer, Aids, Poverty, Differential Equations.

One of the traits of being human is that we like to solve problems.

Fortunately, we're nowhere near having a shortage of them to solve. What if, however, we *could* solve them all? Imagine, if you will, a world with no disease, no poverty, no hate, and no crime. Imagine a world in which terms like *greed, selfish*, and *minority* didn't exist, a world in which everyone lived forever. Imagine a perfect world, a quixotic utopia. Given the choice, would you partake in it?

If life were eternal, would it have a point? Our existence would be dull and void. It seems that while we strive to solve problems, we can't deal with solving them all. We are analytical machines fueled by problem solving, our existence driven merely by the search, the answers insignificant.

A problem for many, death is life's next big adventure. In fact it's the only thing certain in life, save heartache and taxes. Starting in our youth we spend each birthday becoming aware of and counting down to our death. Yet we spend all our resources, if you will, trying to cheat it. We avoid it, prolong it, and in most cases fear it, yet could we live without it? Death begets time's omnipresent importance. Without death, life is meaningless.

Could we humans psychologically deal with such a world? This writer says no. Life without death is tragedy. It's like playing poker and getting a royal flush every hand — not only that, but knowing that you're going to get it before the cards are even dealt. Would you keep playing the game? Or better yet, what would motivate others to keep anteing up? As for me, I'm unsure. I just wanted to use the word *quixotic*.   — **Ryan Jones**

Imagine having 9 million friends, all of whom act, entertain, speak, sing, yell, and dance about every topic possible. A woman wearing a stained white apron hangs out of her third-floor apartment window yelling to the group of kids dancing around a boom box on the sidewalk, "It's 2007! 2007!" It's not 2007, but maybe it can be for just today.

And yesterday, for Christ's sake, can be 1994. We could be driving gray Plymouth Voyagers with missing hubcaps and ripped seats with yellow padding popping out the seams, tapping our fingers on the plastic door rest to Ace of Base. My scrunchie can be blue. Hell, I could be sixteen and healthy, and he could be eighteen and strong, with wavy brown hair and deep brown eyes, his firm hands on the steering wheel, his right foot on the brake and his left foot bare, feeling the softness of the floor mat between his toes while he drives.   — **Lauren Krauze**

The meaning of life is when you make a choice based solely on your own decision, not when you're obligated to because of someone else's view or opinion of your thought, not through an agreed-on choice, but through your own — without permission, but with responsibility.   **— Andrew Robinson**

The meaning of life is to reproduce. Reproduction not only keeps the species alive, but it permits small changes in genes over a long period that allow species to adapt to the environment, gather food, and reproduce more efficiently. This is called evolution. Anything else is simply the result of our cerebral cortex masturbating.

Please note: this doesn't mean that everything else isn't immensely important to humans as intelligent beings — or to any other intelligent beings, for that matter. It simply means that logically, universally, biologically, and scientifically the meaning, purpose, and intention of life is simply to perpetuate it.

— Matthew Polito

I believe the only place you can find the answer to this question is within yourself. How can anyone else tell you what the meaning of your life is? I believe the meaning of my life is to experience all there is to experience in the time I have to do so — from spending time in jail to going to an amusement park, the best and the worst of times. I believe these experiences are all important to my development, and I will never look back on any situation and say, "I wish that hadn't happened." Even while I am experiencing a

trauma in my life I always sit back, think it through, and just let go. I remember that sometime down the line this time will be a memory, so why should I let it control my actions and thoughts now? Too many people take life way too seriously. They have to realize that it is all a passing illusion; it will all end some day, so while you are here you should take your time and use it wisely. Overthinking and worrying are definitely not expanding you as a person; they are limiting your growth and possibly setting you back on your spiritual or personal path.
— **Anonymous**

Confidence is extremely important in living a fulfilling life. No matter what you believe your insecurities are, you should still have the confidence to approach anyone. I know I might not be the best-looking, smartest, and coolest guy out there, but I do know that I will talk to anyone at any time. I would have no problem going up to a beautiful girl and asking her to dance, for her number, or just for a quick chat. If you believe that you can't obtain something, then how are you ever supposed to? If you don't try, you might avoid disappointment, but there's no chance for excitement either. And that is no way to live. Hold your head up high, be friendly and courteous, and when you want something, go for it. There is nothing holding you back except you. Embrace life and be confident! That is the key to a rewarding life.
— **Andrew Vitale**

The meaning of life is there is no meaning. Life in itself is intrinsically worthless and pointless. The only value life has is the value assigned to it by those living. There is no greater plan, there is no basket of kittens, no free pony rides, no Playdough Fun Factory for Christmas at the end. You're organic matter at the whim of a cold and uncaring universe expanding exponentially into nothingness, governed by laws too bizarre to comprehend. You're a son to your father, a lover to your significant other, and food to a polar bear. When you were born you stank, when you die you rot. Worms will crawl in your head and live there. If life had any meaning at all we wouldn't be falling over ourselves to exterminate ourselves in the name of God or country. I wouldn't have to walk down the street wondering if this'll be the day that shady crackhead finally kills me for six bucks. College girls wouldn't have to wake up in a strange bed not knowing where their pants are. If everyone valued life, assigned it a glimmer of meaning, we might be living in a starkly different world.

Life is survival.

We're mindless skin socks moving our genes into the next generation, designed, conceived, and functioning to pass on less than a thousandth of a milligram of genetic material. We're a virus of a different kind. Unless some magical conscious paradigm shift occurs, that's what we will always be. Nothing more. Nothing less.

— **Joe Urchak**

I don't know if I have the right or responsibility to tell everything I know. I don't know if I have the right to intervene or interfere with anyone's sincere investigation of their existence. I don't know if I have the right to criticize someone's awkward attempts. I don't know if I have the right to persuade or shape opinions.

I do know that I have the right to exist, and in doing so, to encounter this universe. I do know that this encounter will have a variety of effects. I do know that some will see, while others only look. I do know that I will never be here again. Therefore, during the time I have, I will teach, learn, criticize, and persuade. My existence is and will be a positive effort, geared to achieve, spiritually, emotionally, and physically that level necessary to maintain a symbiotic relationship with this universe. **— Lionel Robert Ford**

What is life?
Life is a magazine.
How much does it cost?
Fifty cents.
That's pretty expensive,
That's life!

— Bohandy

The meaning of life is to be the eyes and ears of the universe, as Kilgore Trout once put it. It is to treat your fellow human beings as you would want to be treated. Serve others, travel often. Love those around you, and others around you will spread the love like you have. To those who look on your kindness as a burden, do not harden your heart. Or pity them. Love those who want to be loved, but be there for those who may need you later.

The meaning of life? Make life as meaningful as you can. For yourself, for others, and for those who will come after you.

— **Robin May**

My personal meaning of life is not knowledge, but the discovery of knowledge. I like the path of discovery, creativity, and imagination. I always try to help people understand how I have come to my conclusions, why they are better than other solutions, and I am also willing to throw in a few hints here and there to help them out. Sure, we could say the meaning of life is to be happy, but what is it that truly makes you happy?

To make life better, you have to take that first step. Just about everyone knows a few things that they "could" do to get something done. We find reasons not to do it, or we make up some tasks to completely avoid the problem. I have found out that ignoring the first step only prolongs the negative and that I feel so much better after the task is done.   — **Lewis Edward Moten III**

The human being, like any other creature with a complex nervous system, craves constant stimulation. If one could transform this concept into a painting, it would be a painting of a giant nerve ending, always searching for feeling.

Whether it be pain or pleasure, intellectual or physical, we need stimulation. We are always on the lookout for the novel, for something that will appease our neurological structure with the nourishment it needs.

This is why we read books, have sex, ask philosophical questions, play sports, answer philosophical questions, watch movies, have children, take drugs, and do everything else.

The novel is more stimulating than the routine or commonplace, which is why we go on vacations, enjoy a change of pace, buy new clothes, can't stand monogamy, and crave the new.

All this is easy to sum up: the meaning of life is to feel. The flesh is all we have. And through it, we live.

Life is inherently meaningless. But this void doesn't sit well with we who crave stimulation, so we invent something to fill it: God. Meaninglessness is also psychologically difficult for many (though not all) people to deal with. For many, life needs to have purpose. Otherwise, why bother? Thus, religion is born.

Many will rationalize their motivations, but it boils down to a single fact: we are all hungry for experience. — R. J. Mills

To me it means trial and error. Our choices and what we come out with in the end and how we process it and incorporate it into our everyday lives. Life is valuable, and every person has some significance to your existence. I have learned this through trial and error. Close loved ones are an extension of how we view and carry out our lives. Life is growing, learning, understanding, and adapting everyday struggles and truly walking away with a newly profound insight. When we die it is the end for us, but to those around us it is another lesson. Each human being will affect thousands of lives in his or her lifetime.

— **Kenneth Cruz**

The meaning of life is that you try to live as long as you can, and everything you love kills you.

— **Holden North**

The ultimate meaning is to seek happiness. At first many folks might think that happiness has to come from carnal or monetary pleasures — getting lots of sex, money, drugs, or shiny objects. But that's so far from the truth! Life is about being happy spiritually. If you left this world tomorrow, could you say you had lived a productive and sound life? When you are forty-five, can you say you made decisions at twenty that you are content with today? If you're twenty, can you say you are living to be internally harmonious with yourself at age forty-five?

Life is not about being a TV character with whom everything has to be spotlessly perfect or everything dramatically tragic. Life is about how you handle things that are seemingly perfect or tragic. You don't need adventure to be content, and you don't need utter peace and quiet to have serenity.

Life is about balance. In balance you are happiest.

— **Sarah E. Wilder**

I believe the meaning of life is to enjoy what you are doing at least 90 percent of the time. Work will constitute the remaining 10 percent of the unenjoyable. Make sure to value the people around you, your friends, and family, because you can't BS and have beers with a bunch of dollar bills. I think we all have to play the best possible game we can with the cards we're dealt. Sometimes you bluff; sometimes you're all in. — **Chris W. Ford**

The meaning of life is not something to be asked, but something to be experienced. Everything that happens in or around your life is the meaning. Nothing happens for a reason; it just happens. Whatever "meaning" you get out of it is purely up to your interpretation of those events.

Life can be made better if you take time to enjoy it, not necessarily doing something fun or exciting but just taking comfort in the fact that you are alive another day. There are many people who aren't who would like to be. Take better care of your life, and don't worry about what other people are doing. Do not force your own beliefs on someone just because you or a group think it's the better way. Let life take its course, and only act when directly affected.

— **Christopher C. Long**

Life means creating a new smile on Sunday and grabbing onto it during the challenges of the coming week. Life means knowing when to keep quiet even if the opposition is making a lot of noise and saying nothing — sometimes, silence speaks volumes. Life means saying "I love you" to that someone special and believing it with all your heart and soul. Life means keeping your cool when the guy in front of you has to go back and "get that special item on sale," thereby holding up the line. Life means accepting defeat gracefully when the object of your affection admits that she only likes you as a friend — a good friend, but a friend nevertheless. Life means cursing out the other driver who nearly hit you when he's a few miles away and with your window up. Life means sitting through a Lifetime channel "chick flick" when you'd rather watch football, 'cause you love her that much. Life means asking about your boss's health when you'd wished he or she had called in sick.

Life means taking lemons and stomping them until the lemonade spills out. Finally, life means knowing that you won't live forever and accepting that with grace and dignity.   — **Everett T. Ruth**

The meaning of life is to find something or someone in this big ball of mud we call earth that makes us happy and gives us the desire to grow and live another day. There is that driving force that we all need to find, whether it be God, family, friends, and so on. My motivation is *hope*, knowing tomorrow will be brighter, the grass greener, the sky bluer, and the world better. If not for that hope, that motivation, that driving force in all of us, there would be nothing, our existence merely as physical as our bones. I personally believe the purpose of my existence is to leave this earth better than how I found it through spreading the love that I've received over the years.   — **Ramya Sankar**

This is taken from a journal entry from my travels through Europe during the summer of 2003. I was twenty-four years old and searching.

"Be happy," the monk said with a quick smile and a nod. He disappeared as fast as he had appeared on this small, desolate, dirt road to nowhere. Who was this strange being? Better yet, what was

I doing here, and more important, where was here? So many questions, and too many answers — I needed to sit and sort.

Simple solutions don't always lead to simple answers, but fortunately for this traveler, the answers started to become clear with the stars. "Be happy" is what the monk said. So my original question about the meaning of life was answered with an even more cryptic answer: Be happy. So what is happy? More important, once we figure out what happy is, how does it play into the meaning of life? This monk didn't give me a lot of room to figure it.

Happiness is a funny thing. Adults reach it through different means: money, power, drugs, sex, worship, love. But to view happiness at its root is to view it as a child would. Children find happiness in every smile, in every sunny day, in every rainy day, in clouds, in a sweet smell in the air, in animals, in plants, in the ocean, in a hug, in a parent's love — all pure things — before the mind and soul turn on the beauty of the world and begin the inner battle between healthy and destructive. So if this is happiness, how do we all get back? As a transitioning adult, how do I reach back to my childhood for that happiness? Maybe the recognition of this very basic truth is enough to reach back. Maybe. Maybe not.

The monk wasn't trying to give me a cryptic answer. He smiled, gave a nod, and walked on. It wasn't his answer but his actions: the smile and the acknowledgment. He wanted me to find the meaning of life through happiness, which comes in a simple smile. In other words, partake in this life. Smile, bring joy to others, and you will find the meaning. Don't fall asleep in life's waiting room. Smile, and bring that happiness to all. That's the meaning of life.   — **Joe Koller**

perfecting twisting limbs of flesh between sheets of static mesh couples engorge themselves with sweets and sours dripping from each orifice tasting tongues of pinkish muscle running up and down a shivering spine rubbing throbbing rhythm spinning outwards from the velvet vines

inventing sticky embryonic fluid is their meaning for this lifetime two aching bodies dancing intently in a backward forward motion bursts of warmth are beating steady at their hearts and beautiful places with hopes and dreams of their creations beaming up at them with smiling faces   — **Michelle Claire Morse**

The meaning of life is knowing there is no meaning, at least that a human mind can comprehend. Destiny is the only true comprehension we can have of life, as it is the power that controls it. Socrates wisely wrote, "True knowledge exists in knowing that you know nothing. And in knowing that you know nothing, that makes you

the smartest of all." Nothing is small enough to be truly understood by humanity, but we can make an attempt by acknowledging
this fact.   — Jennifer Lynn Miller

Life has no meaning. Everything, including us, is part of the whole
experiencing itself. Life can be compared to a child daydreaming.
Our true consciousness wakes from the dream and dreams again.

— Sharplee

Life is a battle. It is "fought" best by using rationality, hard work,
competition, cooperation, and game theory in everyday situations.
It is "won" only when you are ready to believe that you have won.

— Devashish Kumar

Life is basically a pile of carbon, oxygen, hydrogen, and other
chemicals. Life is very good at creating new piles. This is the point.
It is kind of pointless.   — Daniel Binet

And further, by these, my son, be admonished: of making many
books there is no end; and much study is a weariness of the flesh
(Eccl. 12:12).

Let us hear the conclusion of the whole matter: Fear God,

and keep his commandments: for this is the whole duty of man (Eccl. 12:13).

For God will bring every work into judgment, with every secret thing, whether it is good, or whether it is evil (Eccl. 12:14).

— **Charlie Clem**

If I may quote from Shakespeare's *Much Ado About Nothing*: "Serve God, love me, and mend."

I believe that sums up life right there. I think everyone has to accept that there are higher powers, whatever they be called, than human beings and that to keep order in the universe, worthy masters must be served. If they are worthy, they automatically obtain your respect — and love. The "love me" portion means that we should love one another (not me exclusively!). Love is giving and receiving...it is endless and renewing. And "mend" is the quest we all have to find contentment. It is our coming back into oneness with ourselves so we can better serve and love.

That is the trickiest bit, because lies, like all the good ideas out there, never die. All too often we tell them over and over to ourselves, and we unwittingly engender our own decomposition. Mistruths are the wee corrupting seeds infecting everything. They make us broken, even before we are born. That, however, is another topic for another book (already written — many times over).

If you want to go simpler, I could quote King Solomon the Wise from the King James version of the Bible: "Fear God and keep his commandments, for this is the whole duty of man." Basically, it reads the same way as the first quote, if you are contemplating deeply enough to observe that. "Fear" in this context is to give awe and reverence to. Don't think it's a negative word all the time. The meaning of life isn't all that complicated to sum up. It's just that the simplest things are always more complex than you can possibly imagine. It all boils down to one word. The Greeks knew better and had several words for it. We English speakers aren't so smart, I think. For us it's *love*.   **— Theresa Magario**

I believe the "meaning of life" is twofold: first, to fulfill some worthy purpose that justifies our existence, and second, to oppose cruelty in all its variations at every opportunity. Of course, for some, the "first" and the "second" are the same.   **— Henry Canton**

It's constantly changing for everyone. I myself have changed my definition of the meaning of life as the years have passed, and am continuing to change it as I speak. A death in the family, a loss of a friend or your first love, depression, or simply a beautiful spring day can give you a different meaning of life.   **— Diana Rodriguez**

The meaning of life is rather basic and may sound entirely too obvious. Simply put, the meaning of life is, in fact, to live. Go out there and live; let people know you exist. What kind of life is it to be reclusive, or miserable, or constantly stressed out? With the age of computers and instant access, too many people have become slaves to technology. People would rather talk through instant messaging than on the phone; they actually prefer typing on a screen, without personality or inflection, to actual human contact. That is appalling. Leave your desk, break free of the computer, and as trite as it sounds, take a long walk on the beach, or watch a sunset, or hit the road and simply cruise until you can go no more. Whatever brings you joy, whatever relieves your stress, whatever brings you a moment — even one moment — of pure, unadulterated bliss defines a truly happy life. Life is nothing more than a series of moments; capture them and make each one as memorable and enjoyable as possible.   **— Alec Jorge Calvo**

The meaning of life is to buy things, buy places to put your things, procreate, then buy things for your offspring and places for your offspring to put their things.   **— Rob de la Cretaz**

Just Lucky, I Guess
I love my wife,

and she loves me.
My kids love me, too.
I have my work,
a house with a yard,
and a big, sloppy dog.

— Barkawitz

We were all given a gift: *life*. There is only one chance here, so we need to make it as wonderful as we can, hoping that we will get to a better place. A test is what it really is to all of us. If scientists can't really explain it, then there has to be a better place, with no war and no fighting. Every country should see this, learn to share their God-given treasures with each other. It would be such a wonderful, peaceful place for us all.

Some day, when all of us are gone to our places, maybe we humans will figure it out. God will be expecting that. After all, it is a very simple solution: *peace!*   **— Cynthia Martin**

Seeing, hearing, touching, smelling, tasting, feeling, laughing, and loving — take these away, and you have nothing.

— Douglas Oneschuk

Love. To truly love someone, completely, and to have that love reciprocated in kind. To experience the pinnacle of joy and the depths of sadness that come with giving yourself unconditionally to another and learning about your true self in the process. To see that we all have some impact on the lives of everyone we interact with, no matter how brief the encounter.

I have never felt so alive as when I have been in love.

— **Mark Damon Rychen**

The more we stop to analyze the meaning of life, the more we miss out on life. Love, pain, grief, joy, anger: take it all in stride. Don't fear life. Live it. Stop finding simplified answers to something you may never understand. The more you live, the more those answers change. Stop worrying about figuring everything out and just live. Keeping still while life is progressing is insanity. Don't stop living, go with the flow.

— **Jay Kim**

My own meaning of life begins with the supposition of a creator. For some, this creator could be "God," and for others it could be more of a general "creative force." Assuming this as a given, allow me to continue.

I believe that all that exists, both that which can be seen, like the physical universe, and that which is unseen, at least without the aid of man-made devices, such as the air, is what constitutes the creator. The sum of *all* that exists is what constitutes this creator, and we all are but a part of it.

I believe it is possible that in the beginning, the creator, or creative force, existed only as consciousness, without physical matter. Then, at some point, this creative force chose to experience itself as more than just consciousness, and that is when all that now exists physically was brought into existence. This would be the event that we now know as the "Big Bang."

Following this logically, I believe that the meaning of life is this: life exists as a way for the creator to experience *itself* subjectively. We are all involved in carrying out this gathering of experience and knowledge for the creator.

Biblically speaking, this could be the meaning behind Jesus' words "I and the father are one," as well as many other quotes attributed to him.

This means that we are *all* one and the same. It is only an illusion that we are separate. The sooner the world comes to realize this, the sooner we can begin to work together to heal our differences and come to realize the sheer perfection of what we are: we are the creator, and he is us.

Love your neighbor as you love yourself, for your neighbor is yourself!

— **Michael Lawrence Johnson**

Time passes, as do people, ideals, and beauty. The only thing a person is truly capable of is realizing and accepting who he or she is.

The meaning of life is to understand the self. If you understand why you tick, you understand why everything ticks.

— **Kevin George**

I live in this city on a three-month scheme. That makes me treasure each moment in this crazy life, stay focused, and evaluate each step. I know it could end at any moment, but it won't, because I believe. The thing about this life, especially in this city, is that all you have to do is ask. Put it out there, like a call to the world, and, presto, there it is! The other day I asked for a filing cabinet, and there it was, on the street, two blocks from my house.

I want to share this with the world. Everyone has this gift. My situation makes me sit up and make it happen, and I'm thankful for that. The three-month thing can be a bit stressful. But big things can be achieved in three months. Just decide and believe.

And life can be made better by moving! Movement, dance, is one of the greatest gifts we have. Let's change the world one party at a time!

I will get my visa, and I won't be an illegal immigrant anymore. But you should try the three-month thing!   — **Laura Hames**

I would like to think that if you or I or anyone else had the opportunity to help one person, even a person we did not know, then we will have found the meaning of life. Helping someone in need or helping to better the life of a fellow human being is one of the most rewarding experiences you can have. You do not have to be filthy rich to do the right thing. Showing compassion to other people greatly enriches their life. No matter how small or large the contribution, you have changed them and quite possibly saved their life. Some people think the meaning of life is religious. Others feel it is the accumulation of wealth. While these can be noble achievements, nothing beats compassion toward a person truly in need.

— **Keith Zigmund**

The meaning of life is having the ability to recognize that you do not know anything about the meaning of life.   — **John Shultz**

The meaning of life is not just celebrating your birthday. It requires that you embrace both your birth and your death. It is pointless to ignore the inevitable fact that you cannot live forever. That you'll eventually be forgotten. That everything you've done will eventually be lost. So pass on those things that may be lasting in human society: peace, love, and compassion.   — **Joseph Wisniewski**

Life sucks — but it's a little more interesting than the alternative.

— **Jim Gossens**

Beer, good friends, family, loving what you do and who you are with, looking forward and questing for what you desire, except when there's beer to drink.   — **Tyler Robbins**

It is entirely possible that the human species evolved — over a long process — from the "primordial ooze" supposedly present on earth in the distant past and that there has been no intervention by some divine being that has given human beings a purpose. It would be safe to assume, then, that humans have no goal in life other than to continue their existence. Even with no set goal given to us by some divine power, humans, alone among all species, have the ability to create meaning in their lives. So anything becomes a legitimate option. It would seem more reasonable to say that the *eudaimonia* — Aristotle's conception of a state of flourishing happiness found through a life of virtuous action and contemplation — to which humans should work for should be a *eudaimonia* of *perception*.

If we as humans, with the amount of time we have for contemplation, perceive ourselves as happy, then we create *eudaimonia* for ourselves, instead of striving to reach some goal we do not know the specifics of. There is no mention of quantity in Aristotle's *eudaimonia*; there is only the manner in which to approach it. This is not to say that one should live a life in ignorance, and be happy as such. We should still strive for knowledge, and be happy with what we find on the journey. *Eudaimonia* should be found along the journey, not at the end.

— **Greg Muller**

It has to be love. What else?

When I was young I used to think love was infatuation, plain and simple. That druglike rush when you meet someone. The kick in the ribs, the drama — he'd be in my veins, and I couldn't get enough.

Then reality would seep in. The glitter would wear away and reveal just another person. Human. Fallible. Sometimes dull.

I'd move on. Or pick a fight and make him move on.

The years passed. Life kicked me around a little. It knocked the princess out of me. Gradually I learned the tough and inescapable lesson that love is something you give, not something you fall into.

The falling part is a trick nature plays to get us to mate with each other. The love part is what brings us closer to God.

— **Karen McIntyre**

Connection gives life meaning. It is the human connections to the natural world, to all the world's creatures, and to each other that, combined, make us whole. To make life better, people would be wise to reawaken these connections and to reassign value to the simple continuation of life.

As a woman of African descent, from my vantage point it feels that the world, especially those with the resources to influence world policy, continues to place more value on death than life. More resources are allocated to creating war than promoting peace, to imprisoning people than giving rise to the concrete conditions that would lead to freedom. Information and access to information becomes more and more controlled, as leaders seek to rule unchecked over masses who acquiesce out of ignorance.

Collectively, we need to pull back the lens and realize that there are no individual acts; what I do has an impact on those around me. Greed in one place leads directly to famine someplace else. Indigenous peoples around the world have some things in common: having been unjustly and cruelly displaced from their homes, and a shared understanding of the importance of living in harmony and respect with the natural world. A better world, where the meaning of life was evident, would mean justice for the displaced and renewed reverence for all living beings. People are, after all, just a small part of something much larger.   **— Darice Jones**

The meaning of life is to rebel against all those other lazy carbon atoms just sitting there.   **— Steve Paluch**

The meaning of life is in this sentence.   **— Eric Miclette**

After a life-altering motor vehicle accident — half my life ago this year — I experienced a period of almost a year where I wanted nothing. I desired nothing. I cared about nothing. I went where I was told to go, ate when I was told to eat, and did very little of my own will. This was not forced on me, it was simply a result of realizing that my life would never be the same again and that my future would be filled with medical complications and a great deal of physical pain.

These two things are still true of my present and my future.

However, after shaking myself out of that emotional coma, I've learned what I believe to be the meaning of life.

Just choose to be happy. There's no formula; there's no plan. Just be happy. It is easy for us to forget that we are in charge of our own perceptions. If you choose to approach life's problems with positiveness rather than negativity, then you can be happy. If you choose to be proactive toward life rather than reactive, then you can be happy. Life doesn't happen to you, it happens with you. You are not separate from your life. This does not mean that you have to be an outgoing, cheery person. It's about how you perceive life. Is it a storm you weather or a path you negotiate? The latter approach can make you happy.

If sitting around and watching TV makes you happy — truly and rightly happy — then do it. If climbing a mountain makes you happy, then do that.

— **Ed Gentry**

For life to have meaning you must be aware that there is life all around you. You cannot be disconnected from it. You contribute to it because you are a part of it. From this collective, a single sense of meaning cannot be formed. Life's meaning is a tapestry in which each thread is a path to a unique understanding. For some, this nexus evokes a sense of wonderment and allows their inner light to glow brightly as the life paths of others entwine with their own. For others, like myself, this constant connection with a bunch of mouth-breathing imbeciles is a constant source of frustration that fuels misanthropic fires within. Perhaps, in this very simple way, the true meaning of life is to let the light inside you shine out. Let your light be either a beacon that draws others to share in your life path or a burning roadside flare that warns others to steer clear of you and to stop rubbernecking as they pass the twisted wreck that is your life.   **— David G. Cummings**

Love a good woman. I have been married for seven years now, and I love my wife dearly. Stella was born in Medellin, Colombia, and migrated to the United States about twelve years ago. Her English is sufficient to allow her to work in an office, but she lacks a complete understanding of American culture.

For instance: by now, many people have seen the TV commercials for the discount phone service 10-10-220 featuring sport figures like Emitt Smith, Doug Flutie, and Mike Piazza. One evening while my wife and I were watching TV, one of these commercials came on. This one featured Terry Bradshaw and the 1980s sitcom character ALF. An interesting repartee ensued in which the space alien extolled the value of a dollar in relation to the amount of long-distance airtime it can purchase.

With absolutely no knowledge of 1980s American television or American football, my wife said, "What's with the dog, and why is he talking to that old man?"
— **Ed Violette**

The meaning of life is to simply enjoy it. Introspection can be needlessly painful.
— **Jay Wiggins**

The meaning of life is simple: live. Live every moment as if it were precious, because it is. Every moment is a gift of time, which should be spent wisely, and in the pursuit of making oneself happy. Don't sit around and watch those moments trickle by and fade away. Live life. Enjoy it. When all is said and done, you have to be able to look back on the time you were given and say to yourself, "Yeah, I lived. I contributed. I mattered to somebody." Because isn't that all we really have? If you don't live life, then it has no meaning, and you have missed the point. Smell the roses, taste the wine, and just live. It's the only life you have.
— **Jason Bourgeois**

Taking into account the idea that life may just be the result of entropy, and the ability to continue life through reproduction yet another random occurrence, it seems to me that the only thing one can do to give life meaning is to try to experience as much as humanly possible. What better way to justify the statistical unlikelihood of existence than by witnessing everything our senses can perceive? What better way than to read, study, and learn all that our predecessors and contemporaries have considered? I submit that the meaning of life is to see, hear, touch, taste, smell, and learn everything that life has to offer. The ultimate and absolutely impossible goal, of course, being omniscience.   — J. A. Invergo

There may or may not be a meaning to life. We won't know till we go, and maybe not even then. So it's better to concentrate on now. Now is all we have, and it is constantly passing, now it's gone, but now it's now again. And while there may not be a point, there is a way to make it better — at any rate, a way to make yourself feel better about it. And it comes back to now. We have a chance at every opportunity, every "now," to make a choice, and those choices will affect every other choice we make.

How do we make it better? At every chance, we make the right choice. And every time we make the wrong choice, we should try to make the next one right. What is the right choice? Well, think about it. When do you feel bad? When you hurt someone or lie or hide behind your fears. If you want a better life, don't do that. And when you do, and you most likely will, try not to do it again. Then you won't feel bad. It really is incredibly simple, but it's also the hardest thing to do. It is your mission for your entire life, and it will take you that long to do it.

Make the most of every opportunity, harm as few people as you can in the process, and you will have the least amount of negative times. "There are no problems, only solutions," said John Lennon. If you have a problem, fix it, and you won't have a problem anymore.

There never comes a time when everything is perfect, but our attitude can sure help. Someone once told me to look on myself in the past as a little child, laugh at my foolish mistakes, and try not to make them again. Enlightenment, in my humble opinion, is just a state of mind, wherein we handle every situation that presents itself with all the knowledge we have picked up along the way and realize each choice is a new chance to get it right, till the next one, which is happening now, and now it's gone again, so there's no need to tear ourselves apart from the inside, just try to do it better the next time. The fewer bad things you do, the less bad you'll feel and the better your life will be. It is simple, but if it were easy, we would not need this book. You are the only person who can live your life; no one else experiences exactly what you do, no one else can tell you what's right or wrong for your life, but that means you also get all the blame. But don't ground yourself to your room, just try to do it better next time, which is about to happen right now.

— **Tim Buchholz**

Life can be made better when I'm willing to take a loss. I used to view taking a loss as yet another piece of evidence of my failure to be who I am — someone I thought was forever unworthy. I always felt I was never enough. My strategy was to hide in the roles of wife, daughter, sister, lover — and do my best to be utterly invisible. I agreed to be a service, a doormat, and a piñata, whatever the abusive occasion demanded. Growing up in an alcoholic family creates such profound experiences of all these things, plus the feeling that I should never have existed.

The day came when in desperation I begged the universe for healing from the unbearable pain that had swallowed me. In answer, I received a full-blown "Saturn's return," a term used to describe several years of destroying all one has built in life to create and find the true self. I was willing to pay any price to help me resurrect myself like a phoenix. I didn't realize I would lose everything to a match I lit and threw in faith in the dark.

A few years later, I can see myself solidly in the mirror. I had the courage to change and go through the grief and recovery of giving up on having a perfect childhood and acknowledging a father I never knew, a mother who self-medicated on God, and a divorce from a husband who was living a double life. I trust that when things are destroyed, it's yet another chance for a new creation. I have experiential proof that when I'm willing to take a loss, I'm willing to be in right relationship with myself and rest of the world.

— **Anna Caldwell**

Pebbles in the Pond of Life

Okay, you're sitting and quietly reading this, but I want you to raise your arm straight up in the air. That's right, straight up, like you always wanted to do in the classroom and either did or didn't, depending on your level of self-consciousness. No, I didn't mean self-confidence; I have plenty of self-confidence and self-esteem, yet sometimes I allow my self-consciousness to hold me back. You know, what will people think, that I'm being a goody-two-shoes, yadda, yadda, yadda, and, presto! Before I know it I'm talked out of my impulse to leave the comfort of my routine, get outside my quality problems, and do something tangible for others. Notice I said *tangible*, not incredible, something that should be feasible within my time frame and treasure trove of talents. I believe that talents are like pebbles in our pockets: if we don't throw them into the pond, they accumulate and weigh us down.

Whoops, do you still have your arm up? Sorry, well let's continue: Arm up! Now say, *I can do that!* Doesn't that feel good? I actually did that exercise with a group of forty elementary school parents at the Parent Teachers Group kickoff meeting to drum up volunteers. We had several people sign up that evening, and from then on, whenever they saw me they would wave their hands and mouth those words: "I can do that." I also discovered then that I had the ability to speak to a crowd of strangers and get them laughing, which has been a wonderful gift that I've put to good use in other volunteer positions.

I've learned a lot about life, myself, and other people through volunteer work, and I've managed to make several wonderful friends. Let me tell you that I kicked a good career at a late age and moved three thousand miles away from all that was familiar, especially my friends. I never knew how important they really were to me until we were so far apart. I was with family, which was great, but I knew I needed to build a social circle of my own and I needed to find employment. My job search took me to the Commission on the Status of Women, and on the intake form I answered a question that was to have profound consequences for me: "Can you volunteer at the commission office?" Some little voice inside said those magic words: "I can do that!" It was like taking pebbles from my pockets, throwing them into the pond, and watching the ripples spread out and intersect.

It eventually took twenty-two months to get my life back together, make new friends, and establish myself, but I never gave up and I believe that volunteering saved me and opened up a whole new world of wonderful relationships.

Showing up with pebbles in your pocket is all there is to the art of volunteering. I know, I know, how can you give time volunteering when you can't even find time to take care of yourself? I strongly believe that in some cases one feeds the other. I remember the days and months of feeling just awful and wondering if I would ever feel happy again. One day I chanced across the phrase "happiness is a by-product of service." Now, whenever I get into a funk, I take a trip to the pond and throw pebbles into the water, and I know I'm going to be okay because "I can do that!"

— **P. Eileen Fisher**

A great many people, both good and bad, have influenced my life. Along the way I have had the distinct honor of encountering a few very unique and inspiring folks. I believe if we listen to and try to understand the people we meet, the meaning of life will unfold before our eyes.

My grandfather was one of these unique people. Born at the turn of the century, he could tell incredible tales of the United States in an era of great achievement. His parents, both of Blackfoot descent, named him L. D. His father, a skilled painter, amputated his own arm after dinner one evening in an attempt to stop the gangrene that was setting in due to an unattended splinter. He died four days later of blood poisoning.

A young boy with no father, L. D. became something of a Huck Finn. His life consisted of fishing, hunting, and a passion for the Old West. At age fourteen he jumped a train and headed to the West he loved so much. L. D. lived the life of a cowboy for the next eight years. Riding the range as a hired ranch hand, he worked cattle drives and saw the western plains. He rappelled into the Grand Canyon and rode a single-jug Harley Davidson back to his home in Beach City, Ohio. He was too young for the First World War and too old for the second. He raised three children with his one and only love, Edith. L. D. fished and hunted like a young man until his body could no longer take the stress. He re-created the "Old West," replete with railroads and mountains in his attic, a hobby that consumed a lifetime. He played guitar and juice harp and spun yarns for his grandchildren. He never missed a day of work and retired at the age of seventy-nine.

I share my grandfather's story with you because this man learned the meaning of life and summed it up in one of our last conversations. I recorded many of these sessions, and this excerpt is from the last. As his life was ebbing because of heart disease, we shared many hours. One bright summer day we talked of life —

his, mine, and life in general. I asked, "Old man, what has made your life worth living?"

His reply was quiet and thoughtful: "I have lived a good life and have paid my bills. My house is mine, and I owe nothing to anyone. Your grandmother has been a good mother and wife and I love her. The most important part of my life is the people I have met and the love we have shared. I took advantage of the life I was given and enjoyed all that this world afforded me. I have never intentionally damaged anyone and have helped all that I could. I am living proof that this country allows the opportunity to succeed, no matter what your station in life. I am not bitter about my ancestry and what has happened to our nation; my mother taught me that changes will come and that we must change as well. I have no regrets concerning my behavior or missed chances or lost treasures. I thank God for every moment."

At this he lit a Pall Mall, which grandmother would have frowned over, and became quiet. He passed just twelve days later.

I visit those words often. There is so much to gain from them. Life is free, but to enjoy it may take effort on our behalf. I listen to those who speak, and I wonder how much comes from the heart and how much is practiced. I have the same passion for my life that my grandfather had for his. I embrace the people I encounter and count myself blessed to know them. We give meaning to our lives by living. I will not live as if today were my last day, but as if it were my first. The world is new and untarnished, waiting for me to discover it.   — **Boone Adams**

My pleasures come from the simple things: holding my grandmother's hand knowing that it isn't forever, and holding it even tighter. My admiration for children's innocence and honesty, wondering at what point that changed for the rest of us. An unforgettable piece of advice from a stranger that I can pass along to others. Knowing that the sky will never look exactly as it does at this very moment, that only I have this exact viewpoint, and having the eyes to appreciate it. Struggling to overcome difficulties and then looking back at how far I have traveled. Listening to the wisdom of an elderly or experienced person for free and having the ears to hear it. Acknowledging my faults and being able to humble myself enough to change them. Appreciating a wonderful quality in someone else, and being able to tell them.

Awareness is what makes me live rather than merely exist. My heart is kind, even though it may have been hurt. It only teaches me to love even more.   — **Courtney Suzanne Stewman**

To reproduce DNA. Plain and simple.   — **Luke Mcallister**

The meaning of life essentially is to "do unto others as you would have done unto you." The essence of all religions can be boiled down to this. Life is a school, a place where we learn from adversity. It is up to us to accept this with valor and bravery. We must be compassionate toward all beings who suffer. It is okay to want to achieve, but not at the expense of others, only to benefit the greater good. Right now, life can be made better by improving the environment and stopping global warming. The earth's resources are being used up at an astonishingly fast pace. It is up to us to preserve this earth for our children and grandchildren.   **— Grace Chow**

Evolution is the progressive force of I am that pervades, and is, everything — because it alone understands how to just be. The purpose of life is to evolve into the most harmonious state, while orgiastically experiencing the precious lows and artificial highs on the way.

Jesus was a liberal Jew who advocated caring for the weakest of society and forsaking wealth. He told the story of the Good Samaritan who sacrificed his time, money, and pride to take care of one considered beneath him in society.

The United States must follow the example of those who see the intrinsic value in every individual, such as Jesus, and not those who wage war for profit.

The earth has lasted for 4.7 billion years. Life for 3.7 billion years. Written human history has existed for thousands of years. Our American society we love has existed for just two hundred.

The way I figure it, we progressed from groups of grunting apes to civilizations in hundreds of thousands of years. We went from computers the size of a football field to the iPod in fifty years. Our technological progress is increasing exponentially. Once we all learn to love each other (and enjoy the hell out of life), global cooperation will lead us into the promised land. So what is this plan to ensure global cooperation?

Paraphrasing John Lennon, we must coat political messages in honey. In other words, you have to convince people that it is in their best interests to change, or else they won't. America's destiny is that of the Good Samaritan.

Here's an American recipe for immediate change worldwide: a two-year barrage of information on global peace on every available medium: TV, magazines, Bluetooth, WiFi, Internet, books, pamphlets. Our message is simple and translated into almost every language: "Love, not war. Let's work together to save not only ourselves but also Gaia, our mother planet. War must go. Cooperation must replace destruction. $1 + 1 = 2$ but $1 - 1 = 0$. If we do not work together, we will perish. Love not war."

During these years of the information barrage, America will bring its troops back to its borders, while reinvesting the unspent military funds into a wide-scale transformation of our economy into a sustainable and efficient one. It will halt all expensive military projects such as $2 billion B-2 bombers. The federal government will now be run as a business. It will assume control of the energy industry — and use the leftover military unemployed and those homeless to put Solar Panels on Everything. These nanotechnology-imbued solar panels produce free renewable energy, along with cleanly splitting water into hydrogen for use in automobiles.

Next it will socialize parts of the education and health care systems, to ensure that every citizen in America is raised in a stimulating and healthy environment. Income tax will be eliminated, while a national sales tax will be implemented. Capitalism remains the name of the market, but the energy/health care/education/pharmaceutical industries are radically changed to preserve our country's prosperity. The War on Drugs is replaced by an approach of harm reduction. Drug abuse will be treated as what it is, a social health issue, which will save the prisons for violent criminals. Science will be heavily subsidized, since it is the reason humans can expect to live for almost eighty years in the United States. As applied knowledge, it will be the savior of our land.

Reason and science and knowledge must be the rule of the land. Passion is good, but only when put to good uses, not when defending an imaginary line on a map or a sky spirit who made gays and now hates them.

All humans have the right to shelter, food, health care, and clothing. The rights of the individual trump those of the state, yet when everyone pursues their best option — cooperation — everyone profits.

All empires eventually crumble, but we have a chance in this global information age to elevate human society. In the scheme of things, would you rather be just another corrupt empire or would you rather catalyze positive change?

The alternatives: rampant global warming, destruction of ecosystems, nuclear winters, genocides, violation of human rights, and the extinction of humankind.

Again, the buzzwords are: "Love, not war" "Knowledge over ignorance and prejudice" and "Solar Panels on Everything."

— **Spoe Broderick**

The meaning of life, of all biology, is meaning. That's what living things do: they *mean*. And what they mean is where they are, where they've been, and what they need. Life is about the salient features of the proximal, developmental, and evolutionary environments embodied in the dynamic structure of organisms. You don't just mean what you say and do, you mean what you are.   — **Jonathan Golick**

There is no meaning of life. We're here, that's it. Nothing more. Therefore any search for the meaning of life will yield nothing and will be a waste of the individual's time. So, where does that leave us? What should we do with ourselves while we're on this dusty rock? I believe the answer to this is very simple: have fun, be nice, and learn everything you can. There are so many wondrous things to see and experience that one shouldn't waste time worrying about why we are here when instead we could be exploring the riches this planet has to offer. Pretend that there is nothing after death — who's to say there is — and just try to have as much fun and experience as much as you can while You Are Here. Who knows if you'll ever be back again.   **— Megan Sierant**

We were put on this earth and made differently, just like pieces of a puzzle. The meaning of our lives has always been and will always be to learn to love each other, to put the pieces of this puzzle together to form something stronger than the sum of its parts. We must learn to understand each other and listen without judgment, to learn from each other and not be dismissive of what we don't understand. The meaning of life is very simple. It's the very nature of humanity that makes it difficult. And that, my friends, is why it's taking us such a profoundly long time to get it right. **— David Green**

Personally, I feel that it is my job to learn how to love — not "amore" but "agape." The kind of love that causes you to forgo

judgment and moral rationalizations in favor of promoting kindness. I can do this for the most part with my children and friends.
Now I am working on the religious right. Fortunately, I am only
forty-seven.   — Sylvia Archer

Through formal education and personal experience I have learned
that everything in this universe is interconnected. Everything we
do, don't do, speak, think, and even observe has some impact on
the universe around us. We may never understand how what we do
causes change, but this ultimately makes it incumbent on each of us
to live to the fullest. We must experience all that we can, learn as
much as possible, and in some form pass along everything that
we are. Procreation is not enough; we must each do all that we possibly can to generate change around us. The life force of the universe is based on change. Nothing remains static for long. Good or
bad (which are relative terms), all that we contribute to the universal whole must advance us personally and as a part of this vector
of time.

Despite our vanity in thinking that we as a species are special
and unique, we can leave a mark. The impact will be felt on multiple
levels throughout the universe as clearly as it is felt within our own
hearts and souls. How we bring about change personally and as a
collective global/universal system will depend on how thoroughly

we live and interact during our time in this and perhaps other life spans.   — John J. Siller

Life for me was the ephemeral beauty of the now, experienced by us as a fleeting snapshot of the universe's persistently expressed patterns. To experience the infinitesimally tiny sliver of the All's spectrum to which we are privy is humbling. We observe that ever-present entity that is the sublime paradox of self-awareness, or God.

Now life belongs to the children, but the chain that connects the ancestors to all future expressions of human possibility is a guide rope that connects us all, regardless of our relative positions along the path. Life is the marriage between order and chaos. Self-understanding must be picked up along the way somewhere, even for short-term survival of the species. It could also be argued that "life ain't nuttin' but sex and money," which though poignantly understated, truly expresses the root base needs that we still must fulfill for the survival and propagation of our selfish DNA. That being said, we will always have a conscious choice to improve ourselves as spiritual beings, as well as self-directed evolution.   — Kristopher Flagg

Life is meaningful when we use our ability to question the meaning of life. It is for the sake of the question, not the answers.

— Bagus Tirta Susilo

Every living organism is a variable in a complex mathematical "story problem" that started at the beginning of time. It only seems natural for us, as a cognizant species, to look for the origin and meaning of individual existence. Instead, the irrelevance of our own separate lives appears when compared to the vast, infinite timeline of the universe. What is the meaning of our presence on that timeline? My life and personal experiences are entirely insignificant and unoriginal compared to the sum of the life spans of the entire human race. Would I have a place in the history of humankind if that very history were to span millions of years? Would anyone? As a whole, we don't yet know what to do with ourselves. We may be worthy of a footnote in the story of our little spot in the galaxy, but it remains to be seen. Check back in a few million years. In the meantime, have some babies and enjoy your senses for what they offer — it's all a natural part of the story problem.

— Dan Coker

To evolve, and to evolve the ability to evolve faster. For humans, this means mimetic, or intellectual, evolution, because mimetic evolution is far faster then genetic evolution. Modern science, where ideas compete through experimentation, is by far the fastest form of evolution we've encountered.

As a species, we should focus on using science to understand ourselves and the world, as well as using technology to make our lives better and increase our rate of intellectual evolution. We should try to decrease the percentage of people who are prevented from contributing by poverty or poor education. We should also strive to extend the scientific method to other areas of human endeavor, such as ethics, and free ourselves from the religious mind viruses that oppose a rational investigation of the world.

— **Jeffrey Burdges**

Philosophers, theologians, paupers, and kings and queens alike: we have all struggled over this riddle at some point, and for countless eons. The answer has been sought, with varying degrees of success, in cathedrals, battlefields, and the purple haze of college dormitories the world around.

The question itself says much about the state of our being.

Ontology. The study of existence. Why are we here? (To climb the Darwinian ladder.) What is the purpose of this thinking beast, this social creature who cannot seem to get along with itself? (To do God's will.) Is this all there is? (To love.) A material plane of existence fraught with pain and suffering? (To acquire wealth.) The endless toil of nine to five ending only by the silent vaporlock of a failed heart valve in a cold apartment. (We are a cosmological accident.) Or Maya, a grand illusion. (Chocolate.) An endless cycle of lies and deception broken only by an existential leap that will bring us into our happy place. (Forty-two.)

The question itself points to our disillusionment and unsatisfied desires.

The answer has been shouted with conviction from the pious lips of fundamentalist criers on street corners but has been demonstrated by the silent devotion of an elderly mother caring for her handicapped son. Generals declare it with their manipulation of human war machines, while artists paint it, sing it, and sculpt it from their hearts. Children find it in their comic book heroes, a fireman's helmet, and their fathers and mothers. A baker knows it, pulling the morning's first sweet rolls from the oven with a smile on his face and a line of happy friends and customers at his door.

The answer is plain to see. The question is wrong.

If you have to ask the question, you will never *know* the answer.

The question should not be, "What is the meaning of life," but rather, "What gives your life meaning?"   — **Kevin Canfield**

From the movie *Da*: "The only thing I know for sure is when entering a public restroom the person exiting has the right of way."

                                                        — **Mike Moore**

If we believe that life is without meaning, it also follows that life is not better or worse without meaning. It simply is what it is. One experiences life as one encounters it. Life can't be made better or worse. Lives can, but life can't. — **John Lloyd Miller**

To console a child who is crying, to quell the child's fears and make him or her laugh. This is all that is needed to give one's life meaning. Nothing more, nothing less.

It is our duty to make the world a little better if only for one other person, animal, or plant. To have improved the conditions of another essence, that is the meaning of life. — **Len Probert**

Life is about giving back to people and receiving goodwill. It's about having a shoulder to cry on, a hand to hold, someone to hug and to love. It's about walking through the fields and feeling like you're flying. It's about seeing obstacles as new pathways and not as blockages. It's about opening doors and building open passages. It's about speaking your wishes and granting those you've heard. It's about hidden treasures and shared surprises. It's about a smile instead of a frown, and joy instead of sadness. It's about accepting the not-so-honorable things in life as part and parcel of the whole journey. It's about living. — **Tiara Shafiq**

I'm now what most people would consider "middle-aged." I was religious as a youngster and grew out of it, wrongly or rightly. I'm married to a wonderful woman to whom daily I feel I can't give what she's given me. I try to imagine my future, and I see a gray, amorphous cloud. I regret an entire parcel of occurrences in my past that I couldn't, or through inaction didn't, make good. I'm somewhat cynical about life, and that cynicism grows as I get older, to my own chagrin.

Why the hell am I here? Is there even a reason? I don't know, and I fear I'll never know. I hope someday I will settle into a peaceful acceptance, even if there is no meaning, or reason, for life.

I fear a previous submission about life being nothing more than procreation (and all else wasted effort) is closer to the truth than all others. And I have no children, so even in that I've failed.

— Mike Fisher

Although I don't remember it, I think my first big step toward consciousness, like any other conscious being, was the realization of myself — knowing on some level that I existed, that "I am." Like all babies, I looked at my own hands and gradually learned that they were me and that I was also them.

Many years later, by simple observation of everything around me, I came to learn that for all living things there is a birth, a lifetime, and then death. Discovering a dead bird under a bed of leaves, seeing my father cry on the death of his mother, touching the skin of my newly born baby brother and sister, or even simply looking at the dry trunk of a giant oak that has become the shadow of the fountain of life it used to be. The signs of this cycle surround us; they are everywhere, and we bear them often without even knowing it. All those signs also tell a message people do not always want to hear: Whoever is given life will eventually have to let it go, and that there is no exception to this rule.

As a kid I often gazed into emptiness, lost in my thoughts. So much so that my teachers ended up giving me a nickname — "the moon" — as I was often up there in my head. But never did I gaze so intensely into the night sky and in my own head as the night I was first introduced to the vastness of space. At a school summer camp a young astronomer gave us a brief but interesting speech on our planet, the solar system, the Milky Way, our galaxy, and the universe as a whole. With the magic of a VHS tape he took us back to the moment of the Big Bang, where most people believe it all began. I was riveted, not missing a word, and at the same time my little brain was trying to grasp what those amazing distant worlds could feel like. I was introduced to the fact that billions of living things came before me, and most probably billions will come after. And all those living things together have been preceded by billions of events and billions of years back to the absence of time itself and the death of the last one of those living things will most probably be followed by billions of years and billions of events.

Later that night, lying in my sleeping bag, as I was gazing at the ceiling of the pitch-black dorm room, trying but unable to close my eyes, it became obvious to me that in the grand scheme of all things none of us made any difference to the outcome of it all. I was terrified and fascinated at the realization of my own insignificance. Somehow this grandiose insignificance of myself both in space and time brought me back to the thought of my own death. Most of all, on that night I came to realize that I was going to die myself eventually and that would not change much in this immense universe. Here again, there didn't seem to be any exception.

The next day, listening to the taunts and praise of my schoolmates, I tried to catch a huge bullfrog in a pond. After forcing my arm under a big submerged rock, I finally caught it. He was huge, gooey, and trying to free himself from my grip. As I reinforced the hold of my fingers on its legs and put my other hand over its eyes it stopped moving. I honestly had no idea what I was going to do with it. Although it had stopped trying to free itself, I could feel it breathing and pulsating.

Maybe my mind played a trick on me, but it suddenly felt like he was breathing at the same pace as I. In a flash I felt a surge of empathy for the poor thing. I saw the pond with all the frog's buddies who were sort of looking at us with only their eyes out of the water. My conscience had gotten to me, and I had no choice but to drop the poor thing back in the pond. I got on my knees, and at the moment I started releasing the bullfrog in the water, a strong breeze of wind came blowing on my back, carrying with it the sound of a thousand maple leafs from the trees right behind me. The sound and the wind were the same that I had heard and felt all my childhood, but at this moment they passed through me, reaching almost to my bones. Getting back on my feet, looking in front of me, on the backdrop of the scene was a lake where many of my schoolmates were swimming, many of whom had only their heads out of the water... like the bullfrogs in the pond.   — Mathieu Sylvain

Much to the author's regret, history has phrased the age-old question, "What is the meaning of life?" incorrectly. Instead, and this will come as a surprise to some, we must ask, "Who?"

I stopped by Life's house on the backstreets of Cambridge. Luckily, he was home and answered the door in his frayed and tattered bathrobe. When we settled down for the interview, at an opulently splendiferous Satori table set, Life was decked out in a smashingly elegant blue shirt and hipless Xpressive Jeans.

Author: So, Life, first off, thank you for doing this interview.

Life: Oh, thank *you* for coming here, Evan. I appreciate it.

Author: Bah, it's nothing. [Shuffles a few pages, gets things in order.] All right, now. I'm sure all our readers are wanting to know: How old are you?

Life: I'm forty-two.

Author: No! [Shocked.] You're not! [Pauses, leans forward.] Really?

Life: Hah, hah! Of course not! I'm forty-seven.

[After ten minutes of stomach-busting laughter spent on the floor, the author manages to regain his composure and continue with the interview.]

Author: So, what do you do for a living, Life?

Life: I drive that cart that collects golf balls at the driving range.

Author: And how do you feel your job relates to your — wait, that's you?

Life: Yup.

Author: I *always* try and hit that cart as it goes by. I must've nailed you six or seven times!

Life: Yup. I know.

Author: *Everyone* does that.

Life: [Scratching his head, sighing.] Yeah.

Author: And here I was thinking you were going to crack a Forrest Gump joke.

Life: Well, no.

Author: What do you think your purpose in life is, then, if you just spend your days driving a golf cart around?

Life: Well, um, hey, do you want any milk?

Author: Yeah, sure.

Moments passed to minutes passed to long, grinding hours. I dropped my notebook, made my way to the kitchen, and found that a window was open, curtains billowing alongside. Life had gone out the window and scampered off. My head dropped, and I placed my hands on the kitchen counter, trying to struggle with the layers of metaphors I'd seen, how to make sense of it all, and why on earth Life had buck teeth. Was this a Cartesian principle proven? Did we all need more "dentists" in our lives? And, perhaps most befuddling of all, why on earth was Life's entire kitchen purple?

— **Evan Fleischer**

The meaning of life is about looking for the meaning of life. Yeah, sounds dumb, right? The thing is, there's not a definite answer. As human beings, we're filled with doubts and fears, and because of that we'll always be searching for the things that make us feel more in contact with ourselves and with others. The things that make us feel unique. We'll try to make a difference in the lives of others, so we can feel our time here on earth is not being wasted. So we feel our lives are going somewhere. Life goes on, and sometimes the older you are, the less you understand things. Why is that? Because we complicate things. When we're kids, things are simple. Everything is new. Everything is exciting. So if you ask me again, what is the meaning of life, I'll tell you this: Do the best you can, enjoying every second and every breath as if it were your first, as if it were your last. Stand up every time you fall. Never give up. Learn to love and to be loved. Enjoy simple things, never taking anything for granted. I guess life's an adventure. Some days are good, others are bad. Battles are fought, and some you win, some you lose. But in the end what's important is to know that you gave your best. That no one could break you. That you remained true to yourself. And in the process, that you touched the lives of others. — **Rebeca**

All I want out of life is love. To love — mutually, completely, and without fear — and to have that love revered and respected for what it is. The meaning of life is love. But cheesecake is great, too.

— **Stephanie Koch**

The meaning of life can be derived from the lack of meaning that is omnipresent. Since your life is in effect meaningless — due to the progress of the universe, your statistically insignificant impact on the tiny part of the universe, your eminent death, and the death of everything you know sometime very soon — the meaning of life arises as a very simple observation. To live, to experience, and to enjoy the experience. Because without those three things, life really is meaningless.

To illustrate the point, think of a fruit fly. It will spawn from a larva and die hours later. During that time, the fruit fly's meaning of life is defined by its existence, its actions, and the results of those actions. If it mates, the genetic information is passed on, and the next generation, with a little luck and chance, will continue the cycle. If the fly wastes its time ruminating about the meaninglessness of its existence, the obscurity of the act of spending all your energy trying to mate, why then, it most likely won't mate at all, and that will end that genetic line.

You have just a short amount of time to learn and then do something in life. In a timeline of history, you are but a point, a moment, an instance, and soon it will be over. Better have fun while you can, because soon you won't be able to.

Now, if you think this means just fly around and mate as much as possible, I would argue that's not living but rather avoiding life. Life is a billion possibilities, and one should try to embrace as many as possible.

— Zac Elston

Life can be made better when we learn to look at it through the eyes of a child. Happiness doesn't come from the latest electronic gadget or the biggest bank account. It comes from seeing the wonder of a pink sunset. Howling at the moon with your five-year-old. Leaving baking soda footprints so your child can think Santa Claus visited. Happiness is all the little things we forget to enjoy as we get older. When we all make an effort to remember the little things, then things like road rage don't happen anymore. When we learn to enjoy drinking a chocolate shake as much as a cold beer, happiness will come again. When we learn to be happy with what we have, we'll quit neglecting our family and selves to earn more money only to have more useless things. Happiness is right in front of us. Just take a child to the park to see what I mean.

— **Judy Valdes**

You want to know how to make your life better? A lot of people — people of "faith" — make it their life's work to tell you how you should live yours. Try thinking for yourself instead.   — **John Moss**

We are a species whose brains have evolved over many millions of years with the specific "purpose" of enabling us, as a species, to eat critters faster than other critters can eat us.

Recent cognitive research hints that philosophy, the arts, music, and literature are all functions the brain performs during the periods when the "eat or be eaten" programming is temporarily idle. So is a joyful night at the symphony simply a bizarre trick by Mother Nature?

With organized society, that programming is used less than in caveman days. But even with office politics, that circuitry, though significantly tamed, remains very active. Politics is our answer to war, and the war that has been fought for survival ever since humankind crawled from the swamps goes on to this day in corporate boardrooms, with the stakes being almost as high.

So I wonder whether it is even possible for us to have the slightest hint about what reality is all about. And since evolution isn't actually "purposive," it is unlikely that our minds will ever expand enough to enable us to recognize the ultimate answer, even when it is staring us in the face. It is an unneeded by-product of the need to eat faster than our predators that created this bizarre concept of getting pleasure watching actors reproduce a comedy or a drama. We may fade out as a species not ever having known why we were here. Or what our roles were.

But I am also a religious man, so I believe there is a Supreme Intelligence who guides us and knows why there is something rather than nothing. But, as I said, even if we were told the meaning of life, there is not the slightest chance we could understand it. Was it Woody Allen who, when asked the ultimate meaning of all creation, answered "thirty-eight"?" That may be as profound as it is funny.

As an Episcopalian, I tend to side with the Zen Buddhists, who claim to reach a oneness with reality — reality being something to be felt and revered but never understood. Some physicists say there can never be as many neurons in our brains as there are facts in the universe, so that in itself may be a constraining factor. Throw in emergence, chaos, and other relatively recently studied concepts, and we are even further from developing a working model of the universe.

We cannot even develop a working model of a cold front more than several days in advance. And what of all those modern-day physicists, who sound more like the Zen sages of old when they use chalkboards to prove there really is no "out there" out there?

But we practice philosophy for our own reasons. For some it is entertainment. An infinite jigsaw puzzle. Some in academia see it as an opportunity to lock horns. For others it offers a chance of getting a handle on things and thereby being in a better position to ease our own pain. For some it is just the final "A" needed to get into graduate school.

Here's a thought, however. Bioethicists are pondering the ramifications of a chemical similar to modern-day antidepressants, which will increase chemical stimulation in the pleasure center of the brain. It is not so fantastical that we could do this, and sooner rather than later.

We've all heard the stories of the lab rats who had two levers.

Pushing one gave them food; the other, pleasure. All the rats chose to die of starvation as they endlessly pounded on the pleasure-giving lever.

What if that medication were initially given to the hopelessly depressed, and then to those with terminal illnesses? Would we no longer care about death or fear hunger? Perhaps we would no longer work. Why carry on with the, no pun intended, rat race, when it no longer matters to us if life as a species carries on? What if countless other species reached our stage and simply decided that life was a painful, negative experience and that we were all fighting our whole lives simply to keep our heads above water?

We might come simply not to care about the species continuing. We see the simplicity of peacefully ending it all while we press that proverbial lever. No more frustration over not knowing why there is something rather than nothing. We will no longer have a need for an answer.

I have to qualify all this by admitting I know little about all this speculation I have heard from the experts, and I suspect not too many of the experts do either.   **— Bernard Cullen**

Life is a stream of collective consciousness forming the perfect sentence that will end with an exclamation point.   **— Ray Hom**

Your faith in God, your family, your job, and your personal activities can be a driving force in the "meaning of life" to most people, and I think for me, those things all have a solid foundation in the issue. But I also believe that there is far more to the meaning of life than meets the eye. I believe life is what you make it outside the undeniable will of God himself. What I mean by this is that you have complete control over your life and can make it what you wish, within reason.

I believe each person should take the responsibility to forge their own destiny in life and find what they feel is the true meaning of life for themselves. The meaning of life will ultimately be perceived differently by everyone and could actually be looked at as a sort of fingerprint of the mind because of the varying outlooks and perceptions.

Life can be made easier for everyone by simply relaxing more. Freeing your mind of all obstructions, which is nearly but not completely impossible, can make life easier. Simply attempting to toss aside daily stress such as money, bills, the job, and so on, can make a dramatic dent in making life easier and placing yourself on the road to a happier life.

I know this all sounds easier said than done, and you're right, it is easier said than done. I find relief in the old standby technique of using a hobby to sway my mind from things I find full of stress. Ultimately, wouldn't a stress-reduced life be a "life made easier"?

— **Jay Adkins**

The purpose of life is the drive for constant improvement. Our only obligation on this planet is to be better human beings at Point B than we were at Point A. While some individuals emphasize improvements of body, mind, or spirit, the drive toward betterment is universal. It's the bond that unites us. Only when the will to improve is gone do we see the darker side of human nature: the greed, the hopelessness, the destitution.   — **Matt Wakefield**

You know, it worries me that so many human beings need to have some "higher purpose" in order to lead a good life. Most people lead good lives so that they will get into heaven, or get closer to nirvana, or some other selfish reason. I refuse to believe that we are here on earth simply to prove ourselves worthy of leaving earth. In fact, I refuse to believe that we are here on earth for any set reason at all. We are here because of a long series of accidents that culminated in the creation of our solar system and the spawn of single-celled life on earth. To put it bluntly, we got lucky.

However, this does not mean that we earthlings have no purpose.

After all, I'm sure I would have killed myself before being able to write this if I felt I had no purpose. I feel that the meaning of life is really whatever you want it to be. For me, the meaning of life is simply to enjoy life, to help others enjoy their lives, and to make sure future generations enjoy their lives more than we enjoyed ours. Or, if that seems too daunting, just not to be mean.

No one is watching over us, so we'll have to handle this one on our own. We all must figure out what the meanings of our lives are, and we must not despair just because there is no "purpose" for us set in stone. We will make our own purposes and fulfill them, because after all, this humanity thing is pretty neat, and it will not be around forever. Let's make the best of it while we can, shall we?

— **Matt Flyntz**

The meaning is that we are all living to die, and I have come to accept this for what it is.   — **T. Shamyr Taylor**

In life, there are means and there are ends. The ends are the wonderful moments we experience. The means are the things we do and acquire so that these moments are fully enjoyable. Going to school, getting a job, working hard, buying a home — we do these so we'll be mentally and physically comfortable when those moments arrive that really make us feel.   — **Anonymous**

Why is sugar sweet? What is the meaning of sweetness? All lesser questions of quantification lead to these "why" questions. The meaning of life is not a question to be answered but a journey to be experienced. As to how life can be made better: life is love. From reproduction to sentiment to familiarity, all life is a working out of growing closer and separation. Not mere feeling, but fundamental attachment that is impossible without separation and reattachment.

All religion and philosophy points in this direction, from Christ's turning of the other cheek to the eternal dancing of Shiva and Devi. There is suffering that is only overcome by love in greater measure. Loving, of course, takes many, many forms, and people are often misguided in how to express it. Life can only be made better by becoming more adept at loving. But again, that is a journey to be experienced, not a question to be answered.

— **Mario Bartoletti**

The riddle is the answer to the question. It is difficult to elaborate on such simplicity, but I will do what I can. Many will look beyond themselves for purpose, reason, validation, and other answers to questions they would surely find if they would only accept that life is the journey and that the journey is the point. What is the accomplishment of a goal without the means? Obviously they are one and the same.   — **Brian Lucero**

Life can be made better by not wasting so many years thinking about what has not even happened yet. Too many people base their lives on events that have yet to take place. To fully enjoy your life, you must live your life day by day, do what feels right, act quickly on everything, and take the consequences.   **— Robin Ehrenberg**

Life is senseless. Art is also senseless. Filling my life with artistic endeavors is the only thing that provides me with a feeling of use-fulness. Nothing else — relationships, jobs, spirituality, or even charity — does the same thing for me.   **— James B. Downey**

The traditional Jewish view is that G-d created the world so that people with free will would choose to serve him and appreciate his creation. This obviously involves a lot of work on our part — it is no free lunch.

The meaning of our life is to participate in this relationship with G-d in the way that is appropriate for us. Each person and nation has its path.

Life can be made better by understanding that everything that happens is *hashgacha pratis* (divine providence). It is all happening for a reason. We cannot understand the reason because we only see a small piece of the puzzle. It is still important for us to try our best and to live by some basic laws.

Perhaps by looking at the criteria by which we will be judged in this life, we can see what we should be doing now:

"So said Rava, when they bring a man to judgment they say to him: 1. Did you conduct your [business] affairs honestly? 2. Did you set aside times for Torah [Bible] study? 3. Did you work at having children? 4. Did you look forward to the world's redemption and reason wisely, inferring one thing from another?" (from the Babylonian Talmud, Shabbat 31a).   — Adam Sragovicz

These past few years have been a time of intense reflection for me, since I was in the World Trade Center on September 11, 2001. It's been a difficult journey, but I'm toward the end of it, and I am happy now, especially since I have moved to Austin, Texas. I am 180 degrees from where I was. Think of the presidential election between Kerry and Bush. You had two very stressed sides, surrounded by overwhelming worry on various topics. That's why it was so nasty. People wanted to eliminate the candidate they felt would cause them the most stress. Now, this is a fundamental part of the problem because it would indicate that stress is subjective, so the meaning of life is different for everyone. Because I'm not a religious person and don't feel I need to listen or answer to a higher power, I feel one must answer to what is right within oneself. Again, this indicates that the meaning of life is incredibly subjective. However, I do think it has basic commonalities that could possibly be applied across cultures. (Forgive me if they start to sound like dopey eighties feel-good posters.)

Laughter — it feels good and it's contagious. Don't work too hard — it makes you believe you're doing good, but really you're just robbing yourself of more time for laughter. Be kind — no one likes a frown or getting yelled at. Be helpful — do things for others and expect nothing in return. (I don't do this to feel good or look for payback, I do it because, well, I don't know why, but I do.) Know at least one good joke you could tell to anyone. Cook at least one dish wonderfully — food brings people together and encourages laughter. (Cook with someone, and it's so much more fun; eat with a crowd at home, and it's even better.) Don't worry; it'll all work out eventually. Take big problems in little chunks, it's easier that way. Have no regrets. If you love someone, tell them.

Laughter is the most important part; surround yourself with people who make you laugh. A sense of humor eliminates stress.... Perhaps humor is the meaning of life.   **— Heather L. Thompson**

This question reminds me of a discussion I had with my physics professor about a year ago. We were discussing the sheer size of the universe and how since it is so huge there is a great chance that an exact clone of myself exists somewhere and is doing the exact same things I am doing right now. If this is true, how could there be a meaning of life? If random chance allows for there to be an exact duplicate of me, then would we have the same meaning of life? Trying to answer these questions does nothing but bring society down. I think we should focus on questions with real answers that could benefit us all, instead of engaging in great philosophical debates about how many angels could fit on the head of a pin. Soul searching like this is about as useful as the male nipple, just there to make life look less weird but serving absolutely no purpose. Focus on reality, and great things will happen.

— **Christopher James Iversen**

Just as there is no speed of the sky, no weight of happiness, no batting average of my car, no consensus of the clouds, there is no meaning of life. *Meaning* is not a word that applies to "life."

A quest for meaning is equivalent to a quest for water. It's simply an intrinsic human need. What in other animals would generally be the physiological and mental impetus to find an environment with better food and mating prospects equates in the more advanced human brain with a quest for meaning.

As evidence, consider that no one ever finds the meaning of life — they simply become suitably satisfied by love, children, or career, and these become the outcomes of the quest and human fulfillment of purpose.

So, in summary, if you are ever consistently hounded by long-ings to uncover the meaning of life, it's you telling yourself that something is missing in your existence. Stop reading books about the subject — that's the equivalent of reading romance books when you're lonely. Get out and open yourself up to new experiences. You're being set up for an internal battle with your own desire for security.   — **Peter Davison**

As I approach my fifty-fifth year, I find I've learned several lessons. I have had great fortune follow me through my days, some of it earned, some pure serendipity, and all had a dash of good luck. I just live by several guidelines:

1) Do no harm (unless harm comes to you, then defend yourself as if you were an agent of your god's wrath!).

2) Worry is dues paid on troubles yet to happen (so true).

3) There is little black-and-white, it's mostly gray (hard lesson).

4) People are basically good. If you can count your true friends on one hand when it is time to depart, you are a very rich person.

5) You don't have to be a weatherman to know which way the wind blows (thanks, Mr. Zimmerman).

I'm sure I could think of many more of what might seem like platitudes. But for me, they are far from it. These are rules that govern my existence.

While I know I have many years to go, I do appreciate each moment and give thanks to *my* god, which, by the way, has absolutely no connection or similarity to your "god."

I noticed that the word *god* came up a lot in my writing. I worked for eighteen years in social services. Nearly everyone I encountered who had a spiritual side to their lives faired better when diagnosed with some mental health problem. (In a few cases, however, the chosen religion was the basis of the problem.)

Meaning of life? Don't worry, be happy. Sounds stupid doesn't it? But I smile whenever Bobby McFerrin sings it!   — J. Walker

I ask the reader: Does there have to be a meaning to life? Be aware that the only reason we ask this question is that evolution has made us self-conscious beings, and just because we have the ability to ask such a question does not mean that there is an "answer"; and in my opinion there is no answer. In the end I don't think it really matters what someone says the meaning of life is, or that there is a meaning to life at all. I think the more important thing is that you put meaning into your own life.   — Michael Hindes

I think we have been taught that one must have a goal, some kind of ambition, in order to be considered useful to society. Imagine my disappointment when I realized that the one thing I truly excel at — poetry — is not a huge commodity in the twenty-first century. What can I do with this talent, beyond write greeting cards and commercial jingles? Oh, sure, poetry is an excellent form in which to wax philosophical about things such as the meaning of life, but realistically, practically, poems aren't very useful.

I think that maybe we were all put on this earth to question everything, to look at everything, and to soak up every sight, sound, and smell. I just happen to enjoy putting it all down on paper. Despite its seeming uselessness, I find myself working hard to get all the words right, putting them in the best order, editing, rewriting, and changing the poem's landscape many times over. And in that way, writing is a lot like life itself — it changes, for better or worse; it can frustrate and satisfy simultaneously. It has an endless diversity — whatever your vocabulary can envision, you can write. And, like life, a poem is measured in increments, in small pauses of meter and rhythm and rhyme. Life is measured in months and days and years, and all the while, you strive to do something different, to be yourself and be content.

Repetition in poetry is one thing — repetition in life is something else all together. I am one of nine children, and I've noticed as we have grown older that while we maintain our sense of unity and family, we have each grown into our own selves. We are different from one another. Sharing DNA does not change the fact that we all see life a little differently. All it means is that we all get the family "in-jokes" and we have very chaotic holidays. My life would not be the same without all those brothers and sisters in it; it's part of what sets my life apart from others'.

I think the meaning of life is that by the end of it, you should have lived enough and had enough experiences that your life stands separate from all others. Some of the things that set us apart are things we have inherited, things we cannot change — like the family we are born into. But other things are totally dependent on us, like having a desire to nurture one's talent or skill until it's the best it can be. I know that when I die, I will have lived a life that is unique to me, that can be mistaken for no one else's. I accept those things that I can't change — like a beloved but rather useless talent, and an ever-growing family — and I add to them my own desires, hopes, and dreams. Then, voilà, my own custom-made sense of meaning and purpose, with a lifetime guarantee.

— **Rachel Maldonado**

The appreciation and perpetuation of beauty in all its forms. Life is improved when we expand our definition of beauty. Society is improved when we value another's interpretation of beauty, and finding their happiness is an intrinsically beautiful thing.

— **Conor Buechler**

There is no absolute truth about the meaning of life, only each individual's own truth and reality. That is precisely why the answer to this question is not based in religion, nor can it be the same for every person.

We all face many obstacles, traumas, difficulties. For an increasing number of the world's people, this could mean living in poverty and facing struggles of survival every day. For most people, losing someone you love is part of our reality of struggle.

I lost my mom when I was ten to a fast-moving cancer. Because I am an only child, my father and I were extremely close — best friends, even. Even at that young age I felt so lucky to have such a loving, caring, supportive man for a father. By the time I turned eighteen, he had lost his parents, my paternal grandparents. The following year he was killed in a car accident when I was out of town. The total devastation that ensued was the most difficult, terrifying, painful experience I believe I will ever go through.

Shortly after the accident, a woman who had been a close friend of my parents and in my life since I was six taught me a lesson I have not forgotten. And this is it.

Our lives are about the connections and the relationships we have with people. It is about the bonds we are able to make, what we are able to learn about ourselves, thanks to the people we allow in our lives. Our family, friends, even connections with those living halfway across the world are what bind us to the meaning of life. Every relationship we have offers us an opportunity to learn more about ourselves and grow. We are here to grow — to learn more about ourselves, to explore the world and other people in the gentlest and most profound ways.

Writing this as a twenty-four-year-old, I am quick to realize that I have so much learning still to do, that I will hopefully have many, many years to figure out the "meaning of life." I'm not quite sure my meaning of life will change. The avenues of this exploration might shift from time to time as I seek out new people and new ways to learn, but I truly believe the best things we can do for ourselves — the most rewarding, fulfilling moments of our lives — are spent through our relationships with those we touch and share solidarity with.

— **Eva Silverman**

If I'd been asked this question two and a half years ago I wouldn't have been able to answer, but as of July 12, 2002, the answer, for me at least, is children. More specifically a child, my daughter. Before she was born I had no purpose in life, no aspirations, nothing.

When she was born everything changed. It sounds corny, but the meaning of my life is to make sure my daughter has a happy and prosperous life.   — **Christopher Reed**

The world is truly random, and the wise person avoids the poison of negativity.   — **Jim Hodgson**

The masses are demanding honesty, all the while running from the truth. We do need to face up to our frailties and realize we're *all* dysfunctional beings and, most important, we need to be true to ourselves and allow those around us real compassion. Not the Mother Teresa movie-of-the-week type, but the kind of infectious compassion that people around us not only remember but, by example, pass on.   — **Hilton F. Jones**

On the Way Out of a War Zone: A Dispatch from Colombia

Twilight finally managed to break through night's brutal exchange between the FARC and the Colombian military. In Andalucía, a small river community along a *cuenca* off the Río Atrato, we rattled our way through our morning rituals, bodies still sleeping, minds alert, our ears filtering out the sounds of the jungle for man-made chaos. Weeks of nocturnal combat piled on months of armed actors joined with years of threats, displacements, forced recruitment, and death and more death: a war zone. But this plot of land, this carved-out community on top of a hill surrounded by sugarcane is more than just the space between warring armies. In this soil lives memory's ghost. First words were spoken here. The trees contain the maps to dreams carefully crafted in the once-quiet evenings. On the walls, sounds of laughter and first love are recorded.

This morning we move like mute ants, busy with the work of defiance. Older girl children gather up toddlers and corral young boys into order. Women crowd around an open flame to cook the last bit of food, and the men, the few that remain, tend to the boats down at the river. Visiting human rights activists and academics from Bogotá and the United States dissect time's significance and catalogue the history of what cannot be taken on our journey. Together we defy the universal classifications of war: civilians, noncombatants, or collateral damage. Collectively the women, men, and children of Andalucía, like many of the families who live up and down this river, resist the proselytizing of violence's disciples. This is a Peace Community, one of sixty-four that continue in the struggle to maintain a nonviolent life of dignity in the midst of the reigning chaos of war.

We have little, so we take everything, leaving only the shells of small houses and our souls that live in them. When a military helicopter hovers overhead, the sound of the blade slicing through the sky momentarily disorients us. We congregate at the base of the Peace Community *bandera*, a white flag attached to a pole cut from a long tree branch. The flag is a symbol of all the incalculable ways war has changed life's routine. Widows and mothers of the disappeared have gone through the corridors of Hades's knowledge and earned doctorates in steel-plated truths. Children have learned to restrain their laughter with thick ropes and have developed the habit of reading the invisible script of fear. These are dubious honors.

Forty years ago, peace was driven out of this country. Since then, Colombians have been left with the corpses of soldiers, hollowed-out men and women who have tasted the power to give and take life. Their righteousness is sanctioned by the state or by their ideologies, all of which are fueled by greed. The North and South Americans, the Europeans, Israelis, and the Japanese all have a role in the kidnapping of peace. But here, on the margins of the nation, in a place that is unseen by the eye of the cartographer, we have dared to envision a world of nonviolence. Hope in tomorrows and in our children's tomorrows, faith in the beauty of love and humanity, is what makes us subversive. Our will has made a home of our conviction. Our conviction is worn like an amulet that protects the meaning of our lives. It distills our collective truth. We survive because we find strength in each other. We belong to no place in the world but here.

We begin our descent to the river. We carry our future on our backs. Our eyes are braver than our mouths. They cast us forward into the unknown. Our feet compel us to stay, for this will be the last time they touch the smooth earth of Andalucía. We are heading down river to the Peace Community of Costa de Oro where we will, for now, be safe. Our souls heave with excruciating sobs. Our memories of home drops from our bodies like birth. We are silent. The leaves look on as we pull our boats down the river and whisper their good-byes. The wind dances off the water, taking with it our secrets.   **— Asale Angel-Ajani**

When most try to describe the meaning of life, they accidentally end up describing life itself through some "Chicken Soup for the Soul" anecdote. This fallacy is quite common, for people are always searching for meaning through exemplification, which, in turn, materializes things far more than a question of this nature should allow. Now, I am not a genius, nor am I some kind of nihilist who thinks that the question will never be answered. But I think, for now, the meaning of life is the lack of meaning. Knowing that you don't know gives our lives so much more meaning than a polyester tail pinned exactly on the back end of a donkey. So if your religion, or cute story about how your daughter's first words showed you the true meaning of life, is beautiful enough for you to accept, that's great. But it'll be ambiguity and contemplation for me. That's exactly what gives my life meaning.   **— Ross Res**

Of course, everyone's looking for a last frontier. Something to conquer and call their own. Everyone wants to be a rock star or an artist. Everyone wants their legacy.

And everyone's looking for these things in all the wrong places. All the most impossibly wrong places. Looking for peace and self-fulfillment within, without. Keep tweaking things in your life, keep fine-tuning, have another kid, buy a bigger SUV, get a promotion, and be a damn philanthropist. It's not going to make you feel better. None of it will. It's all Band-aids on a bullet hole.

The only way to live all the way is to live your life as if it were your masterpiece, as if living a grand story, a perfect piece of art, a beautiful song were what you're here for. When you focus on creating your masterpiece, all the minutia fall away, and you see the world like it's meant to be seen: a studio at your disposal.

Quit externalizing creativity with cheap mediums; everyone's originality is all the same when it comes down to paper and percussion. Internalize all you have to give so it bursts out of you at the seams and sweats through your pores until you glow like some angel left on earth.

Until you feel the beauty of silence and yourself and you want to give that to everyone around you. Until you know all the way inside that to deprive the world of your existence is the very meaning of blasphemy.   **— Estella Reuss**

The meaning of life to me is to be the kind of man who makes my mother, wife, and daughter equally proud. (If I have more kids the same applies to them.)   **— Jim Gaffigan**

Kendo and the Magical Noodles

Long ago there was once a boy named Kendo, who, one midsummer, decided to go on a quest to find the purpose of life. Kendo traveled the countryside, going from village to village, asking, "What's the purpose of life?" Many people ignored him, some laughed, and some were even rude. Most said they didn't know.

Toward the end of summer, Kendo arrived at a large market city on a rainy day. Hardly anyone was out, and merchants were closing shop early. On one rainy street Kendo noticed a noodle vendor under an umbrella and rushed over to him for refuge. The noodle vendor asked, "Would you like a bowl of noodles?" Kendo replied, "Actually, I'm just looking for shelter."

"What are you doing out on a rainy day like this?" asked the friendly noodle vendor.

"I should ask you the same thing!" Kendo paused. "I'm searching for the purpose of life."

"Then a bowl of noodles is just what you need," said the vendor. Kendo didn't answer, but the vendor spoke up. "It's on me."

Kendo smiled, and seeing his hunger the vendor handed him a heaping bowl.

"Thank you!" exclaimed Kendo and started to chow down, before stopping abruptly. "These noodles are ice cold," Kendo muttered. "Do you think you could warm them up a bit?"

"Certainly." The noodle vendor handed him a brand-new heaping bowl of steaming, hot noodles.

"Thanks again!" replied Kendo and, noticing the array of spices and oils, asked the vendor, "Can I add some curry and sesame oil, by any chance?"

"But of course," replied the vendor graciously. Kendo helped himself, and after one bite of delicious noodles stopped eating.

"What about the purpose of life?" Kendo asked.

"Don't you see?" asked the vendor. "These noodles are a metaphor. The purpose of life is what you make it."

— Jamie Perkins

My meaning, or my belief, regarding life, is to serve the greater good, more specifically, I serve God — I think. A life without God or some greater good to fulfill is rather pointless. If there were no greater good, this existence, which will eventually come to an end, is to further spread the seed of humankind, and our descendants would exist to further spread. We would exist to exist. It would be circular and ultimately have no meaning. In fact, if all of humankind were to vanish off the face of the earth, it would not matter one bit to anything else but us. If there were no greater good, love and the other beautiful things that poets and scribes have been raving about for millennia would be meaningless as well. I as a person refuse to believe this. There has to be more.

— **Daeho Pak**

Life is half of the cycle of being. Death is the other half. This cycle is repeated time and time again and only stops when a being knows it is time. Each life begins anew, carrying the knowledge of past lives but unable to bring it all to consciousness. There are brief moments of remembrance throughout our lives, but very few beings remember it all. In death we review the previous life's lessons and what we still need to learn. At a time of our choosing, we enter back into life to see if we can become more perfect beings. At a preordained time, we return to death. This cycle continues until we know that we have reached perfection.   — **Diane S. Preciado**

Some of us take life too seriously. We worry so much about what we should and shouldn't do that we don't get to do half the things we'd like. Before we know it, life has slipped by without warning, and we start to panic, because how in the world are we going to fit a lifetime's worth of happiness into the days we have left? Begin to live now, because life is indeed short. Whether you live to be nine or ninety, it is never enough. So have as much fun as you can, while you can.   — **Tabitha Kelly**

Happiness is a disease. At onset, the disease can be rather innocuous — a cool breeze on a sunny day, a stranger's warm smile and kind greeting — but if left unchecked, it can become a serious, life-altering, and highly contagious affliction.

For me, the only purpose in life is to catch as strong a case as possible and spread it to as many people as I can. — **Ryan Schrauben**

The meaning of life is very simple to understand, but is not the grand idea that most people hope will give them clarity and purpose. A grand idea like that would not be the "meaning" of life, it would answer the more prevalent and relevant question: "What's the point of it all?" Now, there's a question I won't touch.

But when asking what the meaning of life is, you are asking

something akin to "what does it mean to live?" That is an easy question to answer for everyone — although most answers will differ slightly, depending on the person.

For me, what it means to live are these things in this order: love, family, friends, fun, health, creativity, achievement, stability, purpose, variety, challenges, excitement. Those things constitute a meaningful life worth living, in my opinion and personal experience.

Is there a universal template? Only within more general themes. Some people might list particular goals, such as climbing a mountain or becoming president. These are moments within greater emotional experiences.

The meaning of life changes every day for each of us: The woman who wants to lose twenty pounds discovers she is ill and will soon try to gain weight. The man who longs for a vacation loses his job. The woman who wants to run a marathon does so, only to feel that she must enter a triathlon to truly feel like an athlete. We set our own bar and meet our own challenges. There are days when an extra $50 in the bank makes you feel like a millionaire and others when the $1.50 ATM charge makes you feel oppressed.

The meaning of life is easy. It's what gives *your* life meaning. It's what you do while you're alive. It's how your time is spent awake, alert, and otherwise. Every day your experiences are like words in a never-ending sentence. You only get limited context, and you'll never see the full body of work.

How can you know the end-all meaning of a story that hasn't finished? The meaning of life is to live, and then to conduct a thorough postmortem once you're dead.   **— Autumn Nazarian**

Give more than you take. Do your best to leave every situation better than you found it. Seek beauty in all its forms. Chase dreams. Watch sunsets. Endeavor to use more than 10 percent of your brain. Don't stifle your deep-from-the-gut, cleansing laughter. Take a moment to ponder the enormity of the universe, then admit to yourself that you can't possibly be the center. Breathe deeply. Swim into the dark water. Let yourself cry when your body tells you to. Love more. Delight in silliness. Don't be bitter. Forgive. Forgive. Forgive.   **— Katy Rhodes**

Operating within the understanding of your own self is the true measure of life and how to live it. If you can be honest with yourself, there is nothing else to life except to enjoy it. If you can look into your own eyes in a mirror without blushing, the world is yours for the taking. I still blush, but every day is a little easier.

— Randolph Potter

We can all grow up, get through school, make the grades, pull through college, and secure that job. But the meaning of life is not the monetary value you receive from that education or work — it is what you leave for the rest of humanity. It is saving that person from committing suicide, not saving money on car insurance. It is assisting the needy in obtaining necessities, not indulging excessive desires. It is inspiring others with your work and talent, not working others to kill their aspirations and dreams, only to fulfill your own. It is to seize the moment, carpe diem, make it all worth it.

The plant of life is a dandelion. With the passing of time, the wind blows the seeds of new life into the air, free to fly into the lives of others, ready to instill its life-giving energy and strength. These seeds grow into new givers, and with time again, will spread their outstretched hands to all the world, creating an inseparable and undeniable chain of love and hope for all to witness. This is the link we all share with each other. No form of hate, prejudice, and separation will ever be able to break that impenetrable nexus of radiance and beauty. This life is only a part of the mysterious but vastly greater challenge of multitudinous frivolous details and worries for the vitality of the new future. We are the creators of the new. We will make the best of it.   — Eric Trabucco

I had a conversation with someone on the Internet today and figured I would share it. This is all me; I've omitted my conversation partner's ideas as I can't speak for him:

It's *doing* something, being there. Even if I fail, I'm good to go. But even if I fail, I did it. That is, I did something.

And there's where we disagree with each other. Your entire life is based on the belief that nothing matters but your relationships. I don't share your belief. In fact, unless you somehow make the history books, when you and everyone you know is dead, your life might as well be pointless. Why bother? Enjoy every minute of what you have, because nothing is guaranteed. That's all that really matters. If you do this with a million people or all by yourself, it's all good.

That you think a person is worthless because they don't share your affinity for interpersonal relationships is laughable.

That's pretty basic, isn't it? What separates us from the animals? So, let's say you fail to have offspring. Hell, let's say the entire human race fails to have offspring. When all the humans are gone, who will care? What will it have mattered? It won't. It's going to happen, everything ends eventually. Unless the Christians are right, the human race will disappear, so even your offspring will fade away. Saying that someone can leave a mark by having children is like trying to leave a mark on a wall of diamond with a single feather. Even if you reproduce, and your line becomes the leaders of the world for the rest of human civilization, when the humans are gone, so what? The earth won't care, it doesn't feel. Even if humans aren't alone, eventually anything a human has ever affected will cease to be.

So do what's important to you right now. After all, the only thing that really matters is what matters to you and applies to you only.

Why does the universe have to be centered on anything? Just because humans have to somehow find a reason to exist doesn't mean the universe follows the same guidelines. Because something follows a pattern (see: relationship) doesn't mean that it is ruled entirely or exists only to fulfill that pattern. Sounds a bit arrogant to me. Unless there is some form of a higher power out there, or a life-form that is immortal, eventually everything that can think will be gone. When this happens, the rocks in space won't care two licks. Even their relationships to each other are unimportant and worthless. What is everything centered on, then? What is the basis for existence? Exactly.   — **Justin Pruitt**

My grandfather once said the meaning of life is to find your work and stick to it. The Buddha said something similar, but my grandfather is no Buddha. Once, staying with him over spring break, I asked, "How would you measure a person's worth, Granddad?"

"A man's worth," he said, "is what you have to pay him for his services."

I wrote a two-page response in verse (I was an aspiring poet at the time) and left it on his desk. Granddad came to me the following evening holding the poem in his hand and said, "Well, Cora, maybe *worth* is more complicated than I made it out to be."

Granddad hates complication. He's a Memphis World War II gentleman, a man whose father beat him for asking "why" too much and whose wife turns down her hearing aid every time he tries to tell her "the way things are." I too have a yen for authority. I want to be able to say, in declarative sentences, this is true, and that is false. I want to be able to say, "Yes! I know why I get out of bed in the morning!" but I don't. The fact is, just when I think I've figured it out, just when that declarative statement is forming in my mouth, my eyes open a little wider and I realize I know nothing, nothing at all.

Granddad's in the hospital now and has been for months. He had a really bad week in November, and my dad and I flew out to see him. Dad brought William Faulkner's *Absalom, Absalom!*, his Bible, and was determined to read the first chapter in the hospital room out loud. Granddad kept falling asleep.

Granddad kept waking thinking of butterflies, saying, "They're just so…delicate," his hand turning in the air and his fingers shaking. "They're so, well, you know, they're just so... some, uh, them only live for a week, ya see."

Last night was New Year's Eve, and instead of going to my friend's house for dinner, or to the Kinky Salon for an all-night sex party, I went to the San Francisco Zen Center. I stared at a white wall, trying not to fall asleep, while the fireworks exploded over the bay and men and women walloped and blew their kazoos in the streets. Before meditation, I drank tea and ate ginger cookies in the dining room with a man who used to be a marine. He and I met a few summers ago at another Zen center, forty miles south in the Ventana Wilderness. When I met him he was bulky and belligerent, always cracking jokes at other people's expense. He's been living at the Zen center for two years now, and last night he was calm and radiant...almost beautiful. It wasn't that lobotomized "Jesus glow" either. It was as if he had looked into the pit of the world, and seen grace and vitriol and compromise and madness and was profoundly and unequivocally okay with it.

I asked him, point-blank, what the meaning of it all was. He smiled and shook his head and said, "I don't think there is any meaning. It just is."

I smiled and shook my head and said, "So what's the difference between that and nihilism?"

He smiled and shook his head again and said, "I don't know."

So we talked of other things. We talked about the city, about the book I've been working on, about the New Year. Then he stood up suddenly and said, "I have to go. I'm jikido tonight," and his black robe fluttered behind him as he walked out the door.

I still don't know any of the answers to any of these questions, but I still hope for answers.

I guess my provisional answer to the question, "What is the meaning of life?" is this: keep asking.

"There's just one thing I don't understand," Granddad said, waking from an *Absalom*-induced nap. "How do they get everything done, in just one week?"   **— Cora Stryker**

Why We Search — An Epilogue

When some of my friends found out I was compiling *The Real Meaning of Life*, I got the same question over and over again: "Why are you doing this?" It was as if I didn't have the right, the cosmic mandate, to ask the big questions unless something awful had shattered my world first. "Did your dog die or something?" "Why do you care so much about the meaning of life?" People half expected me to sell all my worldly possessions — a laptop, a few desk lamps, and a really cool-looking Good Luck Money Tree — and head to a monastery somewhere for deep navel gazing.

Needless to say, I'm not going off to a monastery in Nepal or selling my laptop. I don't know why I care or why so many other people seem to care. Some consider such deep curiosity a gift from

God; others claim it is a by-product of evolution; a few say it is a mere mistake. Regardless of its cause, everyone asks the question at some point. This project proves that. You can be an investment banker on Wall Street or a panhandler in Bombay. Either way, you'll seek meaning at some point in your life. This book raises a lot more questions than it actually answers; it's a damn good thing it isn't an exam prep book, I suppose. After sifting through thousands of entries, you might think I could pick one or two philosophies and cling to them. This is simply not the case. Our world is not black-and-white.

I have come to realize certain things, though. As Einstein once said, "God does not play dice with the universe." So many events in our lives seem random, even cruel. We will experience pain; we will die. And, despite all this, we will also experience moments of blinding clarity when a series of seemingly pointless events comes together to create something beautiful. The discovery of penicillin. Two strangers bumping into each other by chance and eventually getting married. The creation of this book. Each one of these outcomes involves thousands of variables that all must come together just right. Fate, despite all her potential wrath, has an uncanny precision at times. She is a moody artist. You were born. An infinite number of events unfolded in just the right way. You purchased this book, borrowed it from a friend, stole it from the library.

Whatever. Somehow, the book is in your hands. Now it's your turn to write the next chapter.

Enjoy your life to the fullest, do what you truly love to do, and be with those you love as much as possible. Don't let all this philosophical mumbo jumbo bog you down. Don't always listen to the experts. The experts have their own problems; they aren't perfect. Don't worry too much about money, prestige, or permanence. All things come and go: lives, dreams, empires. The ancients realized this. Just have a good time, and you'll come razor close to the meaning of it all, I think. Thank you for reading.

Acknowledgments

There are so many people to thank. First of all, my thanks to the thousands of colorful personalities on the Internet and in the real world who submitted entries. Without you, this book would be two pages long. I am truly grateful. I would like to thank my terrific editor, Jason Gardner, for seeing the project's potential and really believing in it. Mary Ann Casler, Kim Corbin, Georgia Hughes, Mimi Kusch, Munro Magruder, Tona Pearce Myers, and everyone else at New World Library who worked on the book and its promotion. I'm also grateful to those who convinced their friends to submit entries. Thanks, Mom and Dad, for supporting my writing efforts entirely. Thanks to my brother, Evan, for being generally amazing and a loyal companion at the movie theater —

we're serious movie junkies. Finally, I would like to thank the complete strangers who sent me emails of encouragement. To have someone you don't know say that what you are doing is worthwhile is really the ultimate compliment. Thank you, God.

About the Author

David Seaman grew up in Maryland and now attends New York University. When he's not searching for the meaning of life, his other interests include photography, exploring the city, and people watching. He is a contributing writer for the *Washington Square News*. This is his first book.

NEW WORLD LIBRARY is committed to preserving ancient forests and natural resources. We printed this title on Transcontinental's Enviro Edition 100 Natural recycled paper, which is made of 100 percent postconsumer waste and processed chlorine free.

Using this paper instead of virgin fiber for the first printing of this book saved:

- 137 trees (40 feet in height and 6 to 8 inches in diameter)
- 58,112 gallons of water
- 23,370 kilowatt hours of electricity
- 19,848 pounds of air pollution
- 4,721 pounds of solid waste

We are a member of the Green Press Initiative — a nonprofit program supporting publishers in using fiber that is not sourced from ancient or endangered forests. For more information, visit www.greenpressinitiative.org.